RECIPE FOR LIFE

RECIPE FOR LIFE

HOW TO CHANGE HABITS THAT HARM INTO RESOURCES THAT HEAL

GRAHAM KERR AND TREENA KERR

WALKER LARGE PRINT

An imprint of Thomson Gale, a part of The Thomson Corporation

THOMSON

GALE

Detroit • New York • San Francisco • New Haven, Conn. • Waterville, Maine • London

THOMSON

GALE

LIBRARY OF CONGRESS CATALOGING-IN-PUBLICATION DATA

Kerr, Graham.
 Recipe for life : how to change habits that harm into resources that heal / by Graham Kerr and Treena Kerr. — Large print ed.
  p. cm.
  ISBN-13: 978-0-7862-9604-0 (hardcover : alk. paper)
  ISBN-10: 0-7862-9604-6 (hardcover : alk. paper)
  ISBN-13: 978-1-59415-185-9 (softcover : alk. paper)
  ISBN-10: 1-59415-185-7 (softcover : alk. paper)
  1. Christian life. 2. Large type books. I. Kerr, Treena, 1934- II. Title.
BV4501.3.K47 2007
248.4—dc22

               2007018903

Published in 2007 by arrangement with Broadman & Holman Publishers.

Printed in the United States of America on permanent paper
10 9 8 7 6 5 4 3 2 1

DEDICATION

The late William Barclay,
New Testament interpreter, who wrote
these words:

"It is very difficult for any man to judge another man fairly. If we honestly examine ourselves we will see that many motives may affect our judgment. It may be rendered unfair by injured pride

- rendered blind by our prejudices
- made bitter by jealousy
- made arrogant by contempt
- made harsh by intolerance
- made condemnatory by self-righteousness
- affected by our own conceit
- vitiated by an insensitive or deliberate ignorance.

Only a man whose heart is pure and whose

motives are completely unmixed can rightly judge another man — which means to say that no man can."*

*Gospel of John, *The New Daily Study Bible Series,* William Barclay, ed.; vol. 1 (Louisville, Ky.: Westminster John Knox Press, 2001), 193–94.

CONTENTS

7

A PERSONAL NOTE
TO THE READER

You may well remember us from our past celebrity (as the Galloping Gourmet team) rather than know us as we are today . . . as emerging servants. We have heard the word *celebrity* defined as "being well known for being well known" and that a *servant* is one who "responds to the needs of others."

Our story in this book is about the transition from celebrity to servant. We describe it as a little like threading a fine needle with a difficult thread — it takes repeated attempts! We see the needle as our lifestyle choices and the thread as our God-given faith in Jesus Christ. The purpose behind threading a needle is to repair something or to bring two sides together and join them as one — the act, if you will, of reconciliation or the healing of wounds.

We, too, have a purpose. We are able to pursue this purpose because we have threaded our faith through our lifestyle and now we have the resources to be of service, we hope, to you and those you now love or will love.

Past habits that used to harm us have now become resources that may heal others. Our purpose is to sew that seed in your heart and with you to repair our wounded world.

You are about to set out on a journey. If you choose to go from page to page, it will *not* seem to be a direct line of reasoning. This is because its purpose is not systematic but rather sequential.

There are two books. The first seeks to examine the obscured nature of today's cultural "needle" and why it continues to be such a difficult passageway.

The second book tells a personal story, one in which our newly discovered Christian faith *eventually* begins to pass through the eye of the needle using a "seed" idea.

Our journey cannot be told or explained as a "how to" system to be followed to achieve an outcome. It is a sequence born out of a willingness to listen and (according to our gifted seed of faith) to obey.

Our hope is that nothing less could happen to you — that these books would become *one* seed, germinated in your heart and bearing fruit in your life. How exactly this should happen and what then should you do is going to be between you and God! With due regard for the forgoing, we offer our assessment of modern lifestyle choices not in *judgment of anyone* but that it may help us to honestly examine ourselves and, as a result, to work together with others of like mind, not as critics but as contributors to the common good. Only the Holy Spirit can reveal the habits that presently harm you and ultimately limit your ability to love God, your neighbor, and yourself, and only God can illuminate* the specific tragic human needs that could be met by your reordered life.

All we did (and constantly strive to do better) is to listen to that still, small voice within, then to obey its prompting . . . *regardless!* In a microscopic way we have, as a direct result, seen the world become a better place and we are filled with joy and gratitude for having the privilege to be part of God's loving solution.

We continue, in the midst of the occupation until Jesus returns.

— Graham and Treena

*"Arise, shine, for your light has come, . . . For look, darkness covers the earth, and total darkness the peoples" (Isa. 60:1–2 HCSB).

PROLOGUE

Treena and I met when she was ten. I was an older child of eleven. To reenact our meeting for its Biography series on Arts & Entertainment Television, we returned to the place where we first met in Forest Row in the Ashdown Forest, Sussex, in the south of England.

The photograph at left captures the moment that I asked her to stand still for me to take her picture. I'd love to have the original, but I had no film in my camera!

Frankly, I was blown away that this handsome boy wanted to take my picture. I did my best to look as fascinating as any ten-year-old could look in those far-off years.

We met, we fell in love, and eleven years later we married. By the time you read this, we will have been married for fifty years and have been in love for sixty.

We've grown accustomed to *in honor preferring the other* (well, almost!). We have been blessed with strongly independent opinions and our interdependent love. I (Graham) am the forecaster, planner, practical, borderline obsessive/compulsive (?) who takes time to develop an idea and even more time to explain it.

Treena, on the other hand, is immediate, loving, warm, receptive, and always having to wait for me to take a breath so she can get a remarkably intuitive, direction-changing, revelational word in sideways.

This has been my cross to bear; however, I put my foot in my mouth far less often than I would otherwise. Now that I am getting older, I mostly use the coughing interruption as a sign. For years I used to wait until Gra (my nickname for him) took a breath.

Within my prose you will find her sudden arrival in both poetry and prose, bringing her word in season just as she does in our daily life and during our public discourse. I owe so much to her love of life, her absolute commitment to action. Please receive her in *italics* as we share as two people with one purpose: to live our lives as transparent contributors to the common good.

It's all true, what he says about me, even what he admits about himself!

BOOK ONE: THE NEEDLE — OUR LIFESTYLE AND OUR CHOICES AS A NATION

Book 1
Introduction

Salmon, a fishy introduction,
to catch you unawares.
It's a challenge to change or
review your affairs.

Frankly, this is not the kind of book that more or less everyone can embrace like a whole school of herring darting about en masse in the sea. We believe you, our reader, are going to respond in a highly individualistic manner not unlike salmon.

Let's see if you can spot your personality type. While there are six major varieties, we'd prefer to deal in generalities for this exercise.

The Wild Pacific Salmon. The wild Pacific salmon makes a couple of circuits of the ocean before scenting their "birth" stream or river and turning inland. They go from salt to freshwater, stop eating, and begin to use their energy reserves (Omega 3 fatty acids), together with an intense instinct to battle rapids, waterfalls, and hungry bears and go as far as one thousand miles inland, sometimes climbing more than two thousand feet in altitude to reach their breeding ground.

After reaching their goal, they die, having given life to hundreds of tiny salmon who continue to live with the same core instincts.

The Younger Wild Pacific Salmon. Here we have exactly the same instinct to go upstream against the flow except they have only made *one circuit* of the Pacific. They smell the river, they feel the challenge, but they are not ready to *go for it!* They put their desire on the back burner and swim on into their ocean of opportunity until, on the second circuit, they are ready.

The Atlantic Salmon are a bit less radical: they are accustomed to less robust rivers, far fewer waterfalls, and no bears. In their life cycle they may make their way upstream to the breeding grounds two or three times, providing they avoid the anglers! Because of their less-dramatic behavior, they can be "farmed." They are bred in hatcheries, each one vaccinated against disease, and housed together by the thousands, where cheek to gill they are fed with utter regularity. They may vaguely remember their instinct to venture upstream but are pretty well "contained" for the duration — *unless* they find a hole in the nets!

Cod. Now cod are very interesting fish — they simply don't understand salmon. Why go upstream when you can go in and out with the tide of opportunity? There's food to eat and eggs to lay. Why all that drama? And yet the cod stores its Omega 3 fatty acids in its liver, and eventually that liver can have life-giving properties for one of us to consume.

So, which might you be?

Are you the "mature" two-circuit salmon, ready to make a grand dash upstream against all the pressures coming downstream? Or perhaps you get it, but you're not yet ready. You won't forget the idea because it's your core value; it's just not for now.

Or are you being "farmed"? Are you part of the population that knows what upstream means but the pressures and temptations to upgrade have you sidetracked?

Finally, are you baffled by the behaviors I've described? Surely, you reason, life is tough enough to simply live for oneself alone without having to risk life itself for someone else. And oh yes, you pay taxes, and, thus, the government helps others on your behalf

— which is, of course, somewhat true.

The wild salmon's "personality" we call *outdulgence,* and because this is a new word, may we explore its meaning together?

Outdulgence Defined

We define outdulgence as to convert a habit that harms into a resource that heals.

There you have it — a typical sound byte loaded with just enough meaning to be understood, yet short enough to be over-whelmed almost immediately by the next best thing to capture our acquisitive atten-tion.

Our definition runs to eleven words, five of which are seeds linked together by the remaining six. Each seed word has the po-tential to germinate and grow (with use) into trees of understanding capable of gain-ing and holding attention in any competitive landscape.

1. convert
2. habit
3. harm
4. resource
5. heal

It is our intention, in this book, to plant these words in your heart and nourish each word with ten thousand other words that may hopefully give you an understanding and sufficient depth to permit you, for all kinds of reasons best known to you, to begin your journey upstream against truly overwhelming odds.

We are deeply conscious of the great chasm that exists between fact and faith, and we shall attempt to build a bridge between the two by starting to work on the factual, logical side in book 1.

We shall then move on in book 2 to complete the bridge by building out from the other (faith) side until, hopefully, the two sides may join seamlessly in your mind as one idea in search of a better life for us all.

What you choose to do with these five words is entirely your business. Yet this we must say. Whatever you do will be observed by others, some of whom will *instinctively* run with it. Others will need much more time to think it through, and still more may shake their heads and hurry on to their purchase of the next best thing.

Because there is no formal membership of "outdulgers," it will be up to you to share your enthusiasm for the journey with others and, when you find others of like mind, to be an ongoing encouragement to one another. You may even decide to start a small group yourself. Feel perfectly free to do so!

May you be observed as an individual who

- is concerned about others in hopeless circumstances;
- wants to be well enough to contribute to the hopeless;
- understands that some commercial "upgrades" may be harmful to you;
- reviews personal habits *often* to see if any are actually harmful;
- changes harmful habits *without* criticizing those who provide the opportunity;
- adopts creative habits that do no harm to self or others;
- commits any savings of time/money realized through change (on a three-year basis) to those in hopeless circumstances; and
- never, ever, criticizes others who choose not to follow your example.

If you are prepared to be observed as such an individual, then welcome to the river. This year's run has just begun!

CHAPTER ONE:
THE SEED
AND ITS PROMISE

An overworked hill, denuded by need,
Eventually causes a mudslide to speed.
Habits that harm need resources that heal;
Orphans, the hopeless, does this appeal?

On September 18, 2004, much of the city of Gonaives in Haiti was buried by a massive mudslide. More than one thousand men, women, and children lost their lives, suffocated by a mountain that moved suddenly.

It took a lot of effort over many years to move that hillside. More than four hundred years ago, when the area was first settled, the hills were covered in trees, trees whose roots ran deep, trees whose canopies sheltered the earth below.

And then, in their need for charcoal to fuel their simple stoves, the villagers began to uproot their trees and leave the soil without protection. It took years to expose their sheltering hillside and turn it into a sagging monster waiting to pounce.

Tropical Storm Jeanne drenched the northwest coast of the island. Finally the saturated hills could absorb no more. Shifting under its own weight, the mountain suddenly let go. In its slide forward, it turned to a thick, viscous wall of mud that avalanched downward upon the townspeople.

In minutes, it was over. The rain continued to fall, joined now by the frantic tears of those left behind.

To convert these trees to charcoal was a way of life over many years. It was the custom, a commercial necessity; and yet, allowed to go on without restraint, this simple provision led to a disaster.

Have we, in our advantaged communities, so uprooted our economic environment that we, too, are beginning to be buried alive?

Our trees of ethics, virtues, and integrity that provided needed services to others for the common good have been uprooted and converted into free-for-all fuel for modern marketing practices.

What used to be service has become exploitation.

Our communities are becoming saturated as our manufacturers struggle to survive in today's hugely competitive marketplace.

We appear to have too many producers

selling the same goods or services to too few consumers. Only by continually upgrading their marketing message can all these industries survive.

As the messages overlap one another and we consumers work harder and longer to afford to pursue the latest upgrade in our pursuit of the promised benefits, the mountain of our own making begins to slide.

It would now seem that we are reaching our design limits. Even the most alluring upgrades often turn sour and disappoint. For example, as I sit here writing with my mechanical pencil in a spiral bound journal, my wife, Treena, has just hit *that* button on her laptop and lost an entire body of work. Poof! In one nanosecond it's all gone. Another so-called promise hits the dust while I turn the page and slowly carry on!

Ha de ha! I have at this moment spent one and a half hours trying to find how to make the visible marks on a document invisible. It was perfectly simple when I found what I had done. I agree with Graham it can be very frustrating, although I'm not sure how he knows when he is completely computer illiterate! (It must be from hearing me "snort" when something goes wrong!) Yes, I am self-taught. That's what makes it fun! However, I, like many oth-

ers, could not write as Graham does. Imag-
ine twenty-seven books with a pencil and an
eraser! I like puzzles and have always taught
myself everything. I must admit my computer
helps to keep me humble. Does his pencil do
that, I wonder?

Now all of this banter shows signs of the very criticism that we said wouldn't be part of the seeds we have to sow. We should remind you that what we have promised to do is *never criticize without making a constructive contribution.*

So, in place of the services uprooted by exploitation, we now offer the word seeds to be planted while there is still time!

Convert • Habits • Harm •
Resources • Heal

If these seeds germinate, take root, bear fruit, and multiply within our developed economy, then we may not be buried by our saturated mountains of exploitation, but, rather, we could use our harmful excess to fill in the valleys of despair that we so often choose to ignore.

People live in a valley of despair
On your hometown street. Have you seen
them there?
Do you just rush past them hardly aware?

Or simply pass by with nose in the air?
People are chary of human despair.
Will you and I stop on this thoroughfare
With more than just a few coppers to spare?
We could share a smile, our name,
and prepare
To ask for their name to show that we care.
Inquire where they come from — must be
somewhere!
To never have anyone ask for one's name
To be overlooked, ignored, and disclaimed.
While we walk by, this is surely our shame.
America is caring, yet we are to blame!

Our modern-day standard of living depends upon *cash flow,* the continual exchange of money as we provide and pay for our "needed" goods and services. Money must somehow be kept moving. Upon most transactions, we pay taxes, and taxes provide services through public servants. That's the way we get to "enjoy" the so-called blessings of a free-market economy.

Now please compare a viscous flow of muddy money with a swiftly flowing, crystal-clear mountain stream of money. One is thick and oozes along. The other is transparent, and everywhere it flows it brings life, providing it contributes somehow to the common good.

That's exactly how it can be with outdulgence. The money we spend on goods and services that do us harm will sluggishly move forward to suffocate our society. The money we spend on goods and services that bring healing will rush forward to our world, community by community. "The common good will be the good we do in common." And the money keeps moving!

CHAPTER TWO:
BEWARE:
GENIUS AT WORK!

Are we overmarketed, lured beyond reason?
Tempted by "their" genius to seduce?
Turn the other ear. Listen for
compassion's call
To love to give; this can mass produce!

In 1968, Og Mandino wrote one of the most celebrated books on salesmanship: *The Greatest Salesman in the World.* It's a triumphant mix of mud and spring water.

The mud simply adds more volume to the goods and services we consume, sometimes in excess of reason *because* it was sold so well. The clear spring water comes with the strong admonition to always give away half of all you earn to those less fortunate.

By mixing the two so skillfully, it's possible to embrace his principles as *almost* a religious truth. Here are his ten scrolls of wisdom:

Scroll #1   Today I begin a new life.

Scroll #2	I will greet this day with love in my heart.
Scroll #3	I will persist until I succeed.
Scroll #4	I am nature's greatest miracle.
Scroll #5	I will live this day as if it is my last.
Scroll #6	Today I will be master of my emotions.
Scroll #7	I will laugh at the world.
Scroll #8	Today I will multiply my value a hundredfold.
Scroll #9	I will act now.
Scroll #10	I will pray for guidance and I will pray as a salesman.

For good measure, Mandino actually does wrap his principles in a Christian mantle, which makes them sweeter and eventually more profound. The dust settles, and the spring water moves on.

Our world turned its sharpest corner during the seventeenth century, as we entered the Industrial Revolution. Up until then, the goods we used were few, handmade, and almost always utilitarian. With cloth we covered ourselves; with clay we held water, wine, oil, and grain. With iron we cut wood to warm ourselves, to sit on, and eat off. All these items were quite simple and traded at a measured pace. Our possessions (unless wealthy) were few and, for the most part, with them we may have been content. When once we began to mass-produce products, they needed to be sold with greater speed, in greater volume. The hands-on craftsmen became designers who saw their labor performed by costly machines.

Enter the salesman, enter marketing — enter mud? Simple cotton garments become countless shirts and blouses, pants and skirts. The clay bowl or jar is now glass, plastic, or metal, and we own dozens that fulfill the same task. We fill them with food we used to eat and use them to decorate kitchens in which we used to cook. And with the iron we build machines that in seconds replace the hours we used to spend *creating* with our hands.

And now we have time on our hands, and we are quickly bored and need to be entertained.

I agree there are things that make life quicker and faster for little or no reason. Many people have to work hard for just the ordinary modern pieces of equipment and those upgrades, which are getting more and more complicated. They take even more time away from creativity, family, and friends. Caring for others provides so much reward that it is hard to get so bored that we have to go shopping or watch television for hours to get relief.

The stories of generations past told by campfire and candlelight have become page-turning books vivid with imagination and fantasy, and when the reading lacks pace, we turn to the movies. And when they lack pace, we switch on television; and when this fails to entertain, we boot up the PC and dive into its alphabet soup of promised knowledge. And when there are too many conflicting sources of "truth," we finally "activate" the electronic game — an almost perfect mix of fantasy, speed, and our personal mastery of impossible situations. With Game Boy, all things appear possible!

We should not in any way belittle the extraordinary genius that lies behind today's accumulated knowledge of technology and salesmanship. The movement is by far the greatest source of man-made motivation our world has ever known . . . but . . . have we reached (in some markets, at least) a state of saturation?

We have enough clothes to clog the thrift stores as we make room for the next best shirt, and we rent millions of ministorage units to make room for the next best gadget. We create tons upon tons of garbage each day as we discard the wrappings and advertising that surround our next best purchase. All this to keep our metal machines turning as we sit by and watch the ever-increasing need for salesmanship!

I have been tempted by salesmanship. Shoes are my weakness. I've always loved pretty shoes — still do. Graham says I should have been a centipede! Here is my secret to overcome this temptation to buy. I find it impossible to find shoes that are both pretty and comfortable! So, if they are pretty, my feet usually hate them! Then, of course, there is that child somewhere who is going barefoot on stony ground.

Cash flow is the required rational outcome of all this effort, and upon this financial flood our global economy now depends. Many years ago there were fewer machines, and they made products that made sense — things we could justify as *needed*. They were well made and could last a lifetime of domestic use.

Gradually, the salesmen began to experience resistance. "We have a refrigerator, a deep freeze, a clothes washer, a dryer." So, we began to invent the "upgrade" by adding colors and trim and automatic defrosting.

And when that became normal, we began to increase the size. Onward and upward and sideways we went, until the kitchen itself needed to expand. And then the house. All of this required more elbow room as we sprawled out onto farmland and added cars and freeways to help us reach our workplace.

At every turn, there was a salesman. No, I'm sorry. That really isn't true, because in essence we *all* became salespeople as we repeated the unique selling proposition (USP) of the last best thing we purchased.

Then, in order to afford to be sold that penultimate next best thing, we began to be recruited by pyramid schemes through which we could sell our friends on the truly remarkable products that we'd come to *love* after other friends helped us discover them.

That is how we came to rely upon each other — not necessarily as neighbors who cared but as neighbors who cared enough to sell us the next best thing.

Something is telling me we need a little balance here. I have known many friends and strangers alike who have only had the best of intentions to help me when they hear I have a problem of some kind, e.g. diabetes, heart, arthritis. "Drink this, try these pills, eat this vegetable, steam them, or eat only raw veg-etables." Yes, I tried most of them for polite-ness sake, so I could truthfully say I had tried their suggestions. Although some of these things helped me, I was better doing what we had been doing these past years. It's not really the neighbor who is selling; it is the distributor that sells to them. But my, oh my! The cost of some of those supplements is so high! I need to take medications that are proven to work in my life without any apparent side effects. I prefer to choose scientifically based help over that based on hype. I am, after all, capable of making my own choices, as my kind neighbors and friends have made theirs.

This is the way of it. This is the culture of the advantaged nations and the lure for those as yet in development — those millions who have yet to discover harvest gold and avocado appliances and shag carpets, often in matching colors!

Is there a conclusion, a time when we retire our last salesmen, when we all are content with what we have, when there are fewer choices of better things that we really need? Is the best we can hope for a slowing down of the machines, less exploitation by the greatest salespeople in the world as they begin to retire as Hafid, Og Mandino's hero, finally does, only to suddenly become aware that after all the *things* he had sold so successfully, *people* were much, much more important?

In this season of our lives, we can still celebrate the salesman and saleswoman, and the marketing genius that guides their actions. They are bright, motivated, and, yes, here and there they are rightfully convinced that what they sell really is an upgrade, that it does improve the human condition.

Our role is not to criticize; our role here is to try to understand the level of genius at work in modern marketing. Because, if we are to venture upstream against such a torrent of expertise, then we must be equipped with a powerful idea that can provide at least a balance to the greatest sales force the world has ever known.

CHAPTER THREE:
WHICH COMES FIRST: THE
CHICKEN OR THE EGG?

Which comes first, habits that harm
or tender hearts that care?
Oil and water cannot mix, but both are here!

In our case, which came first, our harmful habits or our desire (compassion) to help our neighbor in distress? We suspect that neither, or both, could be the only provable answer. It really depends on the timing.

One of my obvious harmful habits was smoking. I began to smoke because it looked sophisticated, somehow mature, and it came complete with a series of mannerisms that I had observed in others whom I regarded as sophisticated men of the world.

I purchased a cigarette case (leather and gold plate), a cigarette holder in black onyx, and eventually I was given a gold Dunhill lighter and ten thousand Dunhill cigarettes a year in the red and gold tin boxes that I offered at random to other would-be sophisticates in my role as tastemaker, lifestyler, man of influence!

I saw myself in a mirror of my own conceit, and I liked what I saw. Only later did I discover in a dictionary that the derivation of the word *sophisticated* is "to make false." My review of what I observed in others finally ran into another remarkable definition, of the word *humility,* as being "known for who you are."

The genius of modern-day marketing is in its ability to tap into our apparent dissatisfaction with being known for who we are. Almost every message suggests that *their* next best product or service will somewhat upgrade our opinion of self and others' opinions of our appearance and choices.

Of course, the flipside of humility is *pride.* So, perhaps a useful derivation of that word could be a straightforward reversal: "to be known for who we are not."

In my case, with the wonderful gift of hindsight, I've come to see a long, long list of choices all made to somehow upgrade myself in my own eyes. I could take up a great deal of your time to plow through the list of examples and include a slightly fuzzy British bowler hat, yellow pigskin gloves, a silver-topped cane, a jacket with two slit panels at the back (for horse-riding ease — but I had no horse!), a red sports car with wire wheels, Spode china, Waterford crystal, a Rolls Royce, an Alpha Romeo, chateau Lafitte Rothschild (claret), handmade shirts, waterfront homes, swimming pools, ocean racing yacht, and the King of Norway's private dining table and chairs to seat twelve, with twelve complete place settings from twelve world-famous restaurants (we never had time to have dinner!). Oh, yes — and then there were the briefcases, the designer luggage. (The list and, more tellingly perhaps, the reason for the choices will, for some of these things, come later in book 2.) For now it's really enough to let you know that many of the habits that did me and those I love such untold harm had their seed beginning in my desire to be more than I was. Our recent trip upstream has meant that along the way I began to relinquish the "stuff" that obscured who I really was.

Has my change from Rolls Royce to Saturn four-cylinder station wagon been humiliating? Well, yes, to the degree that the condition to which we now aspire is "to be known for who we are."

I am probably a rare bird. Material things have never mattered to me. I just am not attached to things. So, has it been hard for me?

"No" is my truth-filled statement. During my childhood, I had twenty-six homes before we married. I have lived in all sorts of places — by railway tracks, where the train almost came through my bedroom; poor sections of cities, nice homes, nice schools, ugly homes, nasty schools. I became a chameleon and adapted quickly — rich one moment, poor another. Whatever! I'd fit in without question, with mink coats or thrift-shop clothes. Why, you may ask? My father was a portrait painter, so we'd move to where the monied people lived and could afford to have their faces painted for posterity. This work meant that sometimes we had money, but mostly we were poor. Thus I learned what it meant to abound and to be abased throughout my whole childhood. That is the sort of person I am. As long as I'm with Graham and we are happy, living this outdulgent lifestyle we have chosen together, that is all that is important to me.

The great joy in the upstream living of relinquishment is that what we used to spend on appearance or garnish we can now spend on those who simply struggle to survive for another day.

The seed of an idea had dropped into our lives.

Obviously, this is our story and may

have little to do with yours. It isn't meant to. What is important, however, is that *in time* you, too, may reconsider your *present* habitual expenditures of both time and money and ask yourself as honestly as you can, "Is *any* of this doing me *any* harm in *any* way?"

Remember we said, "It really depends on timing." The revelation of harmful habits is a sequence, like peeling back an onion; so often the need to peel is caused by other circumstances, including personal health or finances, as we age or move, as our children leave home, or as the world around us begins to slide off the edge of reason.

Back to the chicken and the egg. Did the habit come first or our compassion for those around us? Several years ago, I had an experience that made an omelet out of the chicken *and* its eggs. It combined habit with compassion *directly!*

I read a statistic in which the United Nations had calculated the number of children under the age of five who died from malnutrition. They were so undernourished that relatively minor childhood illnesses were fatal. The estimate from UNICEF in 2004 was *twelve million children*. This came as such a shock that I almost felt it as an emotional explosion — a blast wave shock of horror at such an enormous loss of life that could be avoided.

Within a day or two, I found myself reviewing estimates of those of us who are projected to die from overconsumption of food just in the United States of America, the undisputed world leader in consumption. The estimate in 2004 by the Center for Disease Control (CDC) was four hundred thousand, and this was later revised downward.*

Statistics can be so dry and lifeless. We hear them used so frequently to manipulate us as citizens, voters, and investors that we simply raise our shields of cynicism and pass them off as yet another gimmick to engage our guilt. And yet, there were the facts: twelve million children and four hundred thousand fellow citizens, all dead — one group through lack, the other through excess!

I almost cried aloud. How could this be? Isn't this, by any measure, an enormous global injustice? Even as I wrestled with what it meant, though, I began to fill sandbags full of excuses to prevent this rising tide of awareness from overflowing into my

*The downward revision in July 2005 possibly was prompted by pressure from parties embarrassed by its size and commercial impact. — GK

personal lifestyle choices. The children died because of choices *their* people made — intertribal warfare, greed, ambition, genocide, no rule of law or democratic opportunity. The food was there; only safe transportation was lacking. All these statements were true, and yet they were not good enough to excuse *my* excess consumption!

This onion-peel experience began our search for a lifestyle of global significance. We could connect our excess to their need, one child at a time if necessary. I say *we* because, in the full meaning of our opening metaphor on the salmon, it is pointless for one fish to find itself one thousand miles up the Frazer River if there isn't another fish with whom to release an abundant new "run" with an instinct to make the same trip their parents made.

Married life needs to be a partnership; we always talk and pray together so we are in one accord. Providing we do this, there is never any need for accusations when things go wrong (which they will — that's life!). Graham and I use this method for all things that pop up in our lives. This makes for contentment and a whole lot less strife. Always be in agreement before making any changes. It helps you avoid arguments in the future. Just a little helpful hint!

It was at this point that the unnamed seed (later to be outdulgence) dropped into *our* hearts. We were confronted with a supreme injustice, yes, but that horror could be turned for good — one couple, one child at a time, until the clear mountain streams became teeming with new life.

Which came first: the habits we changed or the compassion we felt? *Neither came first; they came together.*

Bad habits take no time to absorb us.
Good habits take much longer to form us.
Let's start a good habit and not complain.
By stopping that habit, causing you pain
And your loved-ones to worry,
can't you abstain?
Give to an itinerant family in pain.
Or those out of work,
who endure such shame.
Give to others that suffer in wintery parts,
Leaving mothers to struggle
with weeping hearts
For their starving babies
whose fathers depart.
Willingly give those bad-habit dollars
To the needy, weeping, the downcast,
and others.

We cannot overstress the importance of this overlapping experience because without the two elements being shaken together into an emulsion the habit and the compassion will quickly separate and take on a life of their own. We say this from personal experience!

My undeniably harmful habit of smoking was changed when our daughter, Tessa, at age fourteen offered me her observation: "Daddy, wouldn't it be awful if when you'd finished working so hard and we were ready to sail around the world together as a family, we all had a checkup and a chest X-ray [she was and is, by the way, quite dramatic], and they found that you had lung cancer because you smoke so much. . . ." She paused just long enough to let her clincher bear more weight. "And you died and never got to live your dream."

I really wanted to sail round the world. I'd been wanting to do that since I was fourteen when I sailed small boats in the English Channel. The idea that my habit could wipe out that "dream" was so real that I immediately stopped and never once went back. Had I done that last week and had I been buying those cigarettes over the years, my habitual consumption would have exceeded $1,700 a year.

Back then, in 1970 when the change took place, I was certainly aware of human need and injustice, but I had never been motivated to do anything about it *personally* apart from pay my taxes and assume that somehow, someone, somewhere would handle the problem.

The $1,700 potential took on a life of its own. My health obviously improved, but whatever savings might have been realized were absorbed by the other "things" in my life at the time, not people.

Tessa could have added — and would have, had she been saying it today — "We could look after several poor children at the same price [today's dollars $1,700] you pay out to harm yourself!"

You can do the simple math. We can support a child in Africa for $25 a month, $300 a year. So, for $1,700 — why that's *six* children!

When habit and compassion are considered as one event, the outcome can be truly life changing.

CHAPTER FOUR: FINDING THE FIFTY

A little fifty, find it, keep it, maybe share it?
Go on — spare a dime. It's not a crime!

Saving the world one impoverished, malnourished child at a time isn't such a bad place to start. Children under five years of age are the epitome of the "least of the little ones," especially when their situation appears to be so hopeless.

Today there are several excellent agencies that care for these little ones at the cost of about $28 a month or $336 a year. This covers their education, food, health care, and often religious instruction.

All I would need to do is get Treena to agree with me, and together we would begin to find the fifty cents per day for each of us. Then we'd have $365 for the year, enough to add the postage of letters and simple presents for Christmas and their birthdays.

There are two places to look for the fifty

cents. The first is to examine *very carefully indeed* our actual individual consumption. Is there anything or any amount of anything that might be doing each of us (as individuals) physical harm? The second is to review the larger context of our overall lifestyle. We will get to this later in chapter 6.

At this point we need to state the obvious: Any two people are almost always quite different in genetic makeup and, therefore, can be at markedly different levels of risk when eating the same food.

Treena's parents both died young from heart disease. My mother lived to be ninety. Treena is five feet three and one-half inches tall. I used to be six feet three inches (I'm shrinking!). Treena weighs 128 pounds; I weigh 190. Treena has high cholesterol; I do not. I could go on, but surely that's enough to make the point!

We are different, but we share the same lifestyle, mostly eating the same foods that nowadays do Treena no harm and, as a result, are a good choice for me. At the time of writing in my seventy-first year, I have no need for medication or any kind of supplements. We differ in the *amounts* we eat because of body size and activity, but, otherwise, we have agreed about our shared lifestyle.

Over the past eighteen years, we have carefully searched for those personal fifty cents of potential harm. We've found enough of them to have added up to more than $30,000, all from what we used to spend on food that was not good for us.

We know that you'd love to have some examples. However, we feel strongly that this doesn't actually work well because the moment we begin a long list of specific foods or beverages as potentially harmful to either of us we make that a "bad" ingredient and that's a critical judgment call that need not be true for you! The moment we assemble any kind of list, we introduce the potential for legalism. Frankly, that is deadly to the success of outdulgence, which must by its very nature be free of criticism.

We have been able to work on our food choices by assessing them as TREATS and THREATS. We exclude *nothing,* but we are vitally interested in the *volume.* How much of a good thing is enough? If you inspect these two words, you'll see that they both end in "eat."

THREAT

TREAT

In fact, only the letter *H* separates the two. We see the *H* factor as *H*igh volume and the *H*arm it does.

We have looked very *carefully* at our saturated fat intake and the density of calories. We humans (as a generality) appear to do well when we consume less than 7 percent of our daily calories from "animal fats" that, along with some tropical plant oils, are saturated. Now, let's say that you may maintain a healthy weight by exercising reasonably and eating a total of eighteen hundred calories in any one "normal" day. Seven percent would mean about 126 calories. Since nine calories are contained in one gram of fat, we get roughly fourteen grams (which adds up to about half of one ounce) of saturated fat per *day*.

Now, before you begin to get upset by this, let me add that experts mostly agree that total fats, including those from monosaturated sources like nuts, seeds, olives, and other plants and seafood, can add up to 30 percent or six hundred calories, which is more than two ounces.

So, it seems reasonable (to us in our *careful* choices) to limit saturated fats to one-half an ounce* and "mono/poly" fats to about 2.5 ounces (and by the way, *no transfats* because there now seems to be little doubt that those man-manipulated oils lower the "good" cho-

*A little more for me because of my height and weight and 2,200-calorie limit. — GK

lesterol and increase the "bad" cholesterol and, thus, do nobody any good!).

What all these numbers mean is that each of us needs to come to some conclusion about HOW MUCH we intend to HABITUALLY eat of our TREAT foods (usually calorie dense).

Normal commercial portions have so increased since the late 1980s that almost every commercial serving is unhealthy, thus adding to the rise in obesity and overweight that contributes to the United States deaths attributable to overconsumption. So, *normal* isn't working. Normal could be described as a THREAT, and only you and I can begin to let manufacturers and restaurants know what we consider to be a TREAT by purchasing less.

Now, here is our *essential* point. If we eat less, it costs less, and the amount we save will have two benefits:

- We will be less exposed to risk and, therefore, we may expect to have a health benefit.
- We will spend less on food, and if we assess that *carefully* we will know how much we can give to those whose situation up until now had been considered hopeless.

We have placed considerable emphasis upon the word *carefully* when assessing our actual savings. It may help to explain this in more detail.

A couple of years ago, we noticed on Treena's three monthly blood tests that her bad cholesterol (low density lipoproteins or LDLs) had increased to more than 100. We were aiming for it to be as low as 65 to 70. We looked *carefully* at our purchases. It *really* helps a lot to keep your supermarket receipts and not simply rely upon memory. I often tell people that I have a memory like a steel colander. Everything seems to drain through nowadays, especially when I don't want to face a reality I enjoy!

We found that we were consuming one pound of cheese (saturated fat content) per week. That's sixteen ounces between the two of us, or just more than one ounce per day per person. We cut that back to eight ounces a week, with Treena having less than one-half ounce per day. On the next lab report, her LDLs had gone down to 68, and we had saved eight dollars each month, or ninety-six dollars a year.

When we knew that it was working, we transferred the eight dollars to our out-dulgence account at the bank on the first of each month. In this way, we *know* what we've done to change, and we are measuring accurately the cause and effect both on Treena's (and my) health and our ability to increasingly release resources that heal.

Darling, if I may disagree, from a purely feminine point of view, of course. Gra, that's all very well for you to say in your masculine way. However, some females might not like cheese or don't eat enough of it to cut it down. I did and do go along with you with joy, but that is beside the point. Let me talk about lattes and maybe some of our friends can relate to this a little better. I loved to have coffee time with my friends. I still really like the smell. Yum! It was great to be phoned or phone a friend to "come and have a coffee." Twenty years ago, I was warned that I needed to give up coffee. It was bad for my heart. Now some experts, in fact many, say that decaffeinated coffee is just fine. Dear ones, this is my story; it doesn't have to be yours.

Twenty years later, I was still having problems, and even though coffee was obviously not my friend, I would not give it up, until the evening I spoke at a Mennonite Economic Development Associates (MEDA) fund-raiser for Nicaragua. I remembered the discomfort I had as we drove there in our motor home (named "Gratitude"). I spoke to myself quietly, "OK, OK, OK! I know my coffee habit is costing about fifteen dollars a week, and that's six hundred dollars a year! So, hot water or a cup of green tea and half a nonfat muffin, that would still leave about forty dollars a month, which I could give to these desperately needy farming families. Yes! I will make that three-year commitment." I shared my decision with the audience and made the commitment in front of all those witnesses. And, as they say in England, "Bob's your uncle!" (What does that mean? It means, "So, there you are!")

Do I miss my coffee? Am I tempted? Yes! However, because I made a three-year commitment, the farmers in Nicaragua can be certain that for three years they will get that monthly money. I can't take a cup of coffee, so my discomfort has stopped, and in three years I will be over the habit completely and for good. I feel so blessed to have finally dispensed with the harm being done to my body. Now my money is doing good, where before it was doing no one any good! Yet, today I am helping others and myself. This is a win-win situation. In fact, now one year into this commitment, I seldom, if ever, even think of coffee — just no desire!

But what about the financially advantaged individual who gives millions to those in need every year? Would our idea work for someone who may never shop in a supermarket and who has no need to budget *anything?* Frankly, I don't see how it would *unless* he or she is willing to consider their personal, physical need for less at the same time as someone else's need for just a little more.

When those two benefits overlap in *anyone's* mind, there exists the potential for the cod-like self-interest to become that powerful salmon instinct fully capable of fighting its way upstream against all odds — and thoroughly enjoying the journey!

CHAPTER FIVE:
THE WAIST (WASTE)
EXCHANGE

To waste or not to waist, that is the question?
Our Kit Kat experiment is no autosuggestion.

A great deal has been written about the global rise in obesity and overweight and how the numbers appear to be trending upward almost everywhere. Since overweight significantly increases the risk of hypertension, heart disease, type II diabetes, and some cancers, we could reasonably refer to the condition as a disease in and of itself. What we know about weight gain is that it is almost always caused by consuming more energy than we expend and that the universal answer to this global epidemic is to *eat less and move more!*

Then why doesn't this simple solution work? The answer lies buried somewhere beneath layers of marketing and food technology that collaborate in two main objectives: selling pleasure and convenience; or

"You'll savor the way we save you time!"

To change a food habit or habits that we repeat multiple times a day (almost without thinking) is much more complex than avoiding tobacco, alcohol, gambling, or even drug addition. In each of these cases, you have a *single-issue* focus. But with food — well, you can't just stop eating.

Experts have been quoted as saying that "changing a food habit can be 40 percent harder than breaking a heroin addiction." When I read that, I was frankly skeptical. I've never taken an addictive drug of any kind, so I had no comparison by which to assess the statement. So, I set out my own experiment based on chocolate, which is as close to an addiction as I knew!

I purchased a movie-theater-sized bar of Kit Kat (that extra long pack you can use for piano practice or, presumably, share down the whole row!). I broke it up into fingers and placed these in a plastic freezer bag. On the outside, I wrote what I considered to be my TREAT quantity — a reasonable/ moderate (RM) amount for one day. I set the limit at two pieces and dated it. In two days, the entire bar was gone! I repeated the experiment and used extra willpower. In three days, it was gone!

Now *please* hear me. I do not declare chocolate as "bad" or even as "addictive." All I'm saying is that simply having it in our house overwhelms *my* reason, *my* sense of what is moderate, and *my* willpower. Therefore, I could declare *myself* (NOBODY ELSE) as a chocolate addict and determined that, henceforth, it would not enter the house.

Before Graham made this rather "all or nothing" stand, he was like a truffle hound. He would sniff it out. When I brought bars of chocolate for the children's stockings for Christmas, I was amazed to find he, my beloved, had eaten them ALL! It is nice to have a witness to one's faults, so they say!

Interestingly, I kept my chocolate ban for a number of years until I discovered that I had begun to transfer my response to others and to manufacturers. I was becoming critical of others who ate it and made it! So, one day I had a single piece of very dark chocolate sweetened with Malitol (sugar alcohol). It was OK but didn't lead to a craving. So, today I can claim to be free of the addiction *and* able to enjoy a reasonable/moderate portion.

A word of caution is needed here.
You can only enter into this kind of

experiment with *borderline* addictive foods. Please don't try it with tobacco, drugs, or in some cases with alcohol or gambling. When you *think* you might be addicted, you need professional help without delay.

My having said that shouldn't stop you from looking at the portion sizes you presently eat, especially if you appear to have joined the overweight crowd (a BMI of 25 and above). BMI stands for Body Mass Index, which measurement has been universally accepted as the standard by which we define various risks related to weight.

RISK OF ASSOCIATED DISEASE ACCORDING TO BMI AND WAIST SIZE			
BMI		Waist less than or equal to 40 in. (men) or 35 in. (women)	Waist greater than 40 in. (men) or 35 in. (women)
18.5 or less	Underweight	—	N/A
18.5 - 24.9	Normal	—	N/A
25.0 - 29.9	Overweight	Increased	High
30.0 - 34.9	Obese	High	Very High
35.0 - 39.9	Obese	Very High	Very High
40 or greater	Extremely Obese	Extremely High	Extremely High

Body Mass Index Table

Body Weight (pounds)

Height (inches)	Normal						Overweight					Obese										Extreme Obesity															
BMI	19	20	21	22	23	24	25	26	27	28	29	30	31	32	33	34	35	36	37	38	39	40	41	42	43	44	45	46	47	48	49	50	51	52	53	54
58	91	96	100	105	110	115	119	124	129	134	138	143	148	153	158	162	167	172	177	181	186	191	196	201	205	210	215	220	224	229	234	239	244	248	253	258
59	94	99	104	109	114	119	124	128	133	138	143	148	153	158	163	168	173	178	183	188	193	198	203	208	212	217	222	227	232	237	242	247	252	257	262	267
60	97	102	107	112	118	123	128	133	138	143	148	153	158	163	168	174	179	184	189	194	199	204	209	215	220	225	230	235	240	245	250	255	261	266	271	276
61	100	106	111	116	122	127	132	137	143	148	153	158	164	169	174	180	185	190	195	201	206	211	217	222	227	232	238	243	248	254	259	264	269	275	280	285
62	104	109	115	120	126	131	136	142	147	153	158	164	169	175	180	186	191	196	202	207	213	218	224	229	235	240	246	251	256	262	267	273	278	284	289	295
63	107	113	118	124	130	135	141	146	152	158	163	169	175	180	186	191	197	203	208	214	220	225	231	237	242	248	254	259	265	270	276	282	287	293	299	304
64	110	116	122	128	134	140	145	151	157	163	169	174	180	186	192	197	204	209	215	221	227	232	238	244	250	256	262	267	273	279	285	291	296	302	308	314
65	114	120	126	132	138	144	150	156	162	168	174	180	186	192	198	204	210	216	222	228	234	240	246	252	258	264	270	276	282	288	294	300	306	312	318	324
66	118	124	130	136	142	148	155	161	167	173	179	186	192	198	204	210	216	223	229	235	241	247	253	260	266	272	278	284	291	297	303	309	315	322	328	334
67	121	127	134	140	146	153	159	166	172	178	185	191	198	204	211	217	223	230	236	242	249	255	261	268	274	280	287	293	299	306	312	319	325	331	338	344
68	125	131	138	144	151	158	164	171	177	184	190	197	203	210	216	223	230	236	243	249	256	262	269	276	282	289	295	302	308	315	322	328	335	341	348	354
69	128	135	142	149	155	162	169	176	182	189	196	203	209	216	223	230	236	243	250	257	263	270	277	284	291	297	304	311	318	324	331	338	345	351	358	365
70	132	139	146	153	160	167	174	181	188	195	202	209	216	222	229	236	243	250	257	264	271	278	285	292	299	306	313	320	327	334	341	348	355	362	369	376
71	136	143	150	157	165	172	179	186	193	200	208	215	222	229	236	243	250	257	265	272	279	286	293	301	308	315	322	329	338	343	351	358	365	372	379	386
72	140	147	154	162	169	177	184	191	199	206	213	221	228	235	242	250	258	265	272	279	287	294	302	309	316	324	331	338	346	353	361	368	375	383	390	397
73	144	151	159	166	174	182	189	197	204	212	219	227	235	242	250	257	265	272	280	288	295	302	310	318	325	333	340	348	355	363	371	378	386	393	401	408
74	148	155	163	171	179	186	194	202	210	218	225	233	241	249	256	264	272	280	287	295	303	311	319	326	334	342	350	358	365	373	381	389	396	404	412	420
75	152	160	168	176	184	192	200	208	216	224	232	240	248	256	264	272	279	287	295	303	311	319	327	335	343	351	359	367	375	383	391	399	407	415	423	431
76	156	164	172	180	189	197	205	213	221	230	238	246	254	263	271	279	287	295	304	312	320	328	336	344	353	361	369	377	385	394	402	410	418	426	435	443

Source: Adapted from Clinical Guidelines on the Identification, Evaluation, and Treatment of Overweight and Obesity in Adults: The Evidence Report.

66

Excuse me, I have a question! Does everyone love charts like Graham does? Is it a man thing? I personally have an aversion to them. My brain stiffens, my attitude screams NO! NOT ANOTHER ONE, PLEASE! However, this one seemed to make sense. Not only did it penetrate my resistance, but I put it into practice! It worked! I was (and still am) five foot, three inches tall. I was 155 pounds, and my BMI was 27.

I am now between 128 and 130 pounds, and my BMI is now 20! I am no longer part of the 67 percent overweight and obese (BMI of 25 and above), and I know exactly where I am and so does Sadik (our child who benefits from the donations generated through my change). This chart has been a great help to us both. Please copy the BMI chart on page 34 and you will see where you are today and can change. Yes, you can, if you are willing. If I could do it, so can you! Every so often review the chart, and it will keep you on the straight and narrow.

We would prefer to avoid giving you a list of potentially large portions of foods and beverages because, as we keep on saying, we want to avoid any possibility of product criticism. Therefore, would you please *now* do your homework? It is, after all, *your* life and *your* health and *your* potential neighbor

MY PORTIONS NOW AND FUTURE

#	FOOD/ BEVERAGE	AMOUNT	CALORIES	COST	R/M	CALORIES SAVED	COST SAVED	NEIGHBORS	$ PER MONTH SAVINGS
1	Latte coffee	3 x 16 oz/wk	200 c each	$3.15 each	0	600 per wk	$9.45 per wk	MEDA in Nicaragua	$40.95
2									
3									
4									
5									
6									
7									
8									
9									
10									
11									
12									
13									
14									
15									
16									
17									
18									
19									
20									

in need. So, the benefits are all *yours!*

We also know from *lots* of personal experiences that there is a very strong resistance to compiling such a list because the moment we apply transparent honesty to our daily habits, we can actually measure the outcome. By doing so, we may have removed many of our levels of excuse! Or, perhaps better put, we have begun to peel back the layers of exploitive marketing that led us down their path to excess for entirely commercial reasons.

We entered wholeheartedly into our own assessment because:

- Treena was sick and we wanted her well;
- *Graham was well and didn't want to be sick;*
- We cared about others who were sick or well and wanted to help them help others.

We now know why (and how) we both lost weight and transferred more than $30,000 from our food budget to others in need.

How's that for a double benefit?

CHAPTER SIX:
THE OTHER SOURCE
OF FIFTY

The best of the best, bigger and better;
Houses and yachts, cars and the glitter,
Rewards for success to bring you gladness?
Yes, for awhile. So, why the sadness?

There are, as we have said, two sources of
the fifty. So far we have focused upon daily
cause and effect — those habits that directly
impact our physical health on a day-to-day
basis. Each change may be almost insig-
nificant, but in time the changes add up to
very real health consequences and financial
resources.

The second source may uncover another
kind of "fifty" — one that expresses both
time, money, and even possessions that may
be worth fifty cents, fifty minutes, or even
fifty, five hundred, or five hundred thousand dollars!

These are not so much day-to-day issues
as rather larger decisions where the harm

being done is a lot less obvious and much less measurable. Consequently, the overlapping compassionate connection may possibly change in character. One interesting aspect of the "second fifty" is that, on the surface, it is easily confused with the downsizing that takes place when children leave home to build their own lives. So, why keep the large family home and all its upkeep if we need so much less space?

Downsizing, which happens quite often at the middle- to upper-income level, may not actually result in any financial benefit. Even though the size can be reduced, it doesn't always mean that there is a savings. A major reason for this is that such relatively large amounts of disposable income attract all kinds of excellent salespeople.

The four-thousand-square-foot family home in upper New York State may sell for four hundred thousand dollars. The shift to a Palm Springs condominium of one thousand square feet is certainly less space, but its long list of "upgrades" total — yes, you've guessed it — four hundred thousand dollars, *and* the air-conditioning may cost more than the home heating oil for the larger home. And your new friends next door have done such a lovely job of decorating! And so the "upgrades" take care of any savings you might have otherwise anticipated.

Strange really, I have never been acquisitive. Inquisitive, yes, but not acquisitive. It is nothing to pat myself on the back about. It just never mattered to me. Could it be that I was a perfectionist in all things but never in acquiring perfect stuff? I wanted to be known for me, not my things. In fact, I have bought from thrift stores (close to wealthy people, of course). My mother had always said, "With good shoes, handbag, and gloves, you can make anything look nice." She was right. That is why (as I have already confessed) I have been a female centipede as far as shoes are concerned. Gloves, I have one pair. Handbags, yes and no. I'm getting better, aren't I?

It's good to be a witness. Yes, you are getting much better!

Is it possible to downsize and save? We believe it can be done; to do so, however, may well mean a considerable lifestyle shift because your choice may not *appear* to be an upgrade. In our society the "American Dream" (as variously interpreted by worldwide marketing geniuses) is by nature a *visibly* obvious series of upgrades, even though they actually have little to do with either function or happiness.

Our own journey, which we relate in book 2, illustrates these choices quite well, but it properly belongs as part of a sequence that is only helpful if read in its chronological context.

We can tell you, though, that as we write this book we are residents in a manufactured home park in Mesa, Arizona. We have a corner lot within an extremely well-kept village of more than eight hundred units. The park is for fifty-five-year-olds and above — a sort of Denny's Grand Slam Breakfast community. The most expensive "new" park models available cost about thirty thousand dollars for roughly eighteen hundred square feet. Monthly fees run to four hundred dollars. We moved our RV onto an empty lot next to Ernie and Mary and their very cute cocker spaniel, Buffy. They have lived here for the past sixteen years and are avid square dancing aficionados at *eighty-one* years of age. They are also very kind, very loving people — great neighbors!

What is a good neighbor? What is their creed?
To be simply aware of desperate needs,
To care for those far away and next door.
To feel compassion leap at heart's core,

With weeping, loving hearts for the poor.
Are we such a person? Or do we ignore?
And hide behind self-protection's door,
Time's of the essence; my money's in shares.
I cannot withdraw it, but truly, I care.

The "village" has a fine community center that shows movies on Saturday night and holds potlucks and other seasonal gatherings. It has a lovely heated pool and, well, the list goes on.

We are happy here, we are productive, and we can't help but ask ourselves the very tough question: why not move in permanently?

Our first response has to be *climate*. We arrived in October when the summer's heat had dissipated and left us with the fall/winter/spring temperatures between sixty and eighty degrees — perfect for us because Treena especially doesn't do well in hot or humid settings.

So, why not go north in the summer in our RV and have this as home base for the winter? If we did this and sold our home in Washington State, we might realize a savings of more than five hundred thousand dollars, as well as an annual upkeep/tax savings that could exceed the RV's total expenses!

Our next level of consideration is *appearance*. I'm really sorry to have to put it second, even ahead of our friendships in Washington! Surely people should come first!

To try to explain this awful admission, we do need to let you know that this RV is our thirtieth "home" in fifty years of marriage. During that time we've lived all over the globe, including twelve locations in the United States alone over the past thirty years. One consequence of that mobile lifestyle is that we have dear friends in many places! Each time we moved, we really didn't surrender the value of friends in the old place as people we loved and who graciously loved us back.

Real friends truly do stay in touch. If they don't, they have either lost one's address or we have forgotten to let them know it! Occasionally, friends cry when we leave. Sometimes they know it is right for us, but they still cry. It is tough because it forces you to leave part of your own heart behind. Periodically, I envy people who have lived in one or two places all their lives. They have school reunions, which sound like such fun. They have friends with whom they lived much of their lives. Yes, it might be a delight. I went to thirteen schools and lived in four countries and twenty-nine homes before I married. We have just moved into our thirtieth home since marriage. It does get a little more difficult when one gets older, but there are always compensations. We make new friends wherever we go. All friends, old and new, are important, so we always keep in touch. Don't WE, Gra?

OK. That heavy nudge told me that I need to catch up, *fast!*

So, appearances are a major consideration. We have a single-wide across the street from us for sale by the owner for three thousand dollars, with two bedrooms, one bath, and about eight hundred square feet. Our other neighbor has their washer/dryer outside on

Graham and Treena's present home

76

the deck. Another, in fact several others, have somewhat sun-faded artificial flowers in plastic pots stuck into crushed red rock weed-suppressive landscaping. But it's all very clean and fresh and neat and quiet, and almost nobody externally upstages anyone else.

It's also thirty-eight years old, and the water comes through galvanized pipes that occasionally break. The telephone lines also suffer an occasional delay or interference, but cell phones work just fine.

So, why not?

And here is surely the biggest hurdle of them all: "How then shall we live?" This is *not* your average decision. This is a cultural contest! This is where we believe that the outdulgence idea really helps. It's not *only* about us and our feelings. It's also about that five hundred thousand dollars and what it could do as a resource for others in desperate, *hopeless* circumstances.

It is *so* much easier to see where twenty-five dollars a month could help than half a million. It's easier because we can see, feel, and accurately measure its benefit to our lives (weight loss, cholesterol lowering, etc.) and see the same money bring *life* to a child and know that child by name. It truly *is* a double benefit!

If we invested the half million, we *may* receive 6 percent interest, or thirty thousand dollars a year, and that could bring life to three hundred children, or maybe provide drinkable water for a village somewhere or low-interest loans for struggling farmers.

The problem with larger sums lies in our selective vision of the world and *our* future in it. This, it seems to us, is broken down into a series of steps determined by income/cash flow. This diagram on page 79 may help.

Each step up in income/cash flow has a tendency to fashion its own view of the future. Income/cash flow often comes at the expense of close relationships. Genius demands focus and then the continuity needed to see the opportunity reach its goal. We call CEOs *certified entrepreneurial opportunists*. Their minds are forever scanning their field of endeavor looking for the next best chance to succeed.

Minds like these find it hard to spend much time carefully considering their own children's need for consistent loving attention, let alone the needs of the poor and dispossessed of the world.

One can either trust in the future or fear the future. We are both blessed to be able to trust the future, and thus we have no fear of it. As

Visions for Our Future

$$$ UPPER INCOME

Retire, travel, investment, cash?

$$ MIDDLE INCOME

Retire, move, cash, health care?

$ WORKER INCOME

Work, stay put, house taxes, health care!

¢ WELFARE / DESTITUTE / HOMELESS

Next meal, shelter

WANTS

$$$, $$, $

Neighbor in need?

NEEDS

We "see" the future according to our wants until we move to the edge of our privileged space and see the future according to another's needs.

---

far as I am concerned, I love change and new adventures. However, there are many people, especially women, who feel the opposite. They fear they will never make new friends. In fact, they grieve for friends left behind. This can take a year or so to overcome, and just as they settle, they may have to move again. Children adapt very quickly if their mother adapts. If she doesn't, it can make it very hard for all of them, including, of course, the husband, who is trying to absorb all the intricacies of a new job. Graham has never had this problem with me, and our poor kids just had to adapt. Our family relationships could have come apart by the constant moving for success. I am so grateful we survived.

Success at the expense of close relationships causes some of us to seek at least some reward for all those years of effort. So why not indulge in that ocean-racing yacht, summers in the south of France, a Mercedes convertible, a day at that relaxing spa, with dinner at the latest (and greatest) Chez whatever?

Why not? Because if we did, we'd need the cash flow, and for that we'd need the investments, and for those to grow we'd need to keep on looking out for the next best chance to succeed.

There appears to be no end to the reward-generating lifestyle. Boats get bigger, houses larger, cars more European, restaurants more chic, wines a better vintage, cheeses more aromatic, pullovers softer, swimming pools warmer (and emptier), and everywhere people who call you "sir" and "madam" because you tip so well.

And if I were not to make a substantial lifestyle choice, then three hundred children might die and a village might continue to drink from a polluted stream and the homeless would still wonder about shelter and their next meal.

At each step up in the income/cash flow, we have the choice to gaze steadfastly at the horizon of our personal future or to risk going to the edge of our privileged space and taking a look to see where there may be some obvious need or injustice that literally tears at our spleens. That view may distract you from providing exclusively for your own future long enough to *carefully* consider your place in the overall scheme of things.

Might it be that your choice of home, car, clothes, entertainment, vacations, or RV vehicle represent a habit that harms you? You may well ask, "How could *anything* that provides so much pleasure and satisfaction and reward do me any harm?" To which we may reply, from many pain-filled years of experience, "Are you happy?"

CHAPTER SEVEN:
AN EXIT MARKED PEACE

Being noised by "rock," seeing
media in the raw,
promoting sex and greed.
Think, be honest, does TV, news, computers,
give you rest and peace?
Don't you see our time's essential to those
who are in grievous need?
Serving brings both joy and peace,
which amazingly meets all the need.

There are, the last time we checked, 1,440 minutes in every day. Some things don't change, even though time does seem to be shrinking!

Oliver Wendell Holmes, the famous American jurist, once said, "I wouldn't give you a fig for simplicity this side of complexity, but I would give my life for simplicity on the other side of complexity."

This observation has had a profound effect upon my life over the past dozen or so years. I'm constantly challenging myself to be more productive, to get today's quart of life into my one-pint bottle. Clearly, I'm not alone. Just listen to the marketing messages that promise to make life easier, to save us valuable time — so many ways to release us to have more time for the things that matter most: spouse, children, friends, people in need!

And yet, in an odd (perverse?) way, most of these nifty notions seem to rob us of the very time they promise.

I need to confess right here and now that I felt I was being foolish to resist having a high-speed connection to the World Wide Web. So I signed on and bought an expensive laptop and began the enormously time-consuming task of converting myself to this remarkable series of inventions. It proved to be "simplicity this side of complexity" — a huge source of frustration, an economic waste of time, and, therefore, in my opinion, certainly not worth a fig.

In my life, I want to put complexity *behind* me and to be, as a result, less confused about what I need to do about life and those for whom I care. Frankly, I need clear, uncluttered time to *think,* and so far the modern age of communication and media have been so intrusive that we begin to look like hermits in our efforts to retreat from their constant interruption.

VANITY IN A VACUUM
people, people, people, people
people everywhere,
people talk in circles
sometimes in a square.
chatter, chatter, chatter, chatter,
chattering causing crime,
chatter people, people chatter
tongues in overtime.
minds seem blank with idle chatter
eyelids rarely blink.
people, people, chatter, chatter
too engrossed to think!
people chatter, chatter people
chattering life away;
futile chatter, barren people,
wasting every day.

"Simplicity on the other side of complexity" has a more resounding benefit to our ears and our hearts. We open up our cell phones for an hour *after* our lunch has digested. We return and receive our calls *after* we've given our morning's *best* to the work at hand. We put off interruptible work until the afternoon. We chat about our personal relationships over all meals, and we choose *never* to listen to media while we eat. We had found ourselves becoming cable television news junkies and feeling more depressed by the volume of critics who filled our airtime. We decided to read a good newspaper and listen to the BBC World Service and NPR. At least that gave us time to think in more depth than the typically sound-bitten rehash of yesterday's conflicts.

We have gained roughly three hours per day — more than one thousand hours a year! The more time we won back from the complexity of today's media communication and electronic connections, the happier we became *and* the more connected with people!

Mesmerizing evil eye,
vortex sucking all vitality
Numbing creativity,
all proclivity and sensitivity.
"My program's on!
I can't talk now.
Pretend I'm out or in the bath."
Friends' company is vanishing fast.
Farewell the happy "O come in."
The pleasure of a friendly call.
That drop-in. The knock on the door.
Where have they gone?
Do they still care?
Do we? Does it matter after all?

It seems to us that the quality of life, what we've come to call the QOL Factor, has more to do with time than money. Certainly, it can be argued that having enough money makes it possible to "buy" time, or a more peaceful environment, but we've discovered that these "oases of peace" are mostly images we download from advertising. We live in a crowded, bustling world, and genuine peace is hard to find during normal "business hours," especially if we are concerned about our personal success at — well, at anything that focuses upon the indulgent *me*.

This, again, is where outdulgence comes alive. Outdulgence is not about me — at least not about the acquisitive me. It's much more about other people who might benefit because I'm less self-focused.

Several years ago, in an attempt to better use my time, I went down to the local "soup kitchen" that fed about four hundred homeless and destitute people each day. I asked the lady in charge if perhaps she needed some onions chopped (I do a mean job of speed chopping). "I think you have a more vital contribution to make," she replied. "I need someone who will sit and talk to my customers."

Her customers were homeless, quite a few of them deeply medicated. Most needed a good bath, let alone a meal. I wasn't at all sure I could do it. I mean, how do you strike up a conversation? I was way out of my depth.

But I did it. I mussed up my hair, took off my tie and jacket, pulled my shirt out a bit, selected a table of only two people, and sat down.

My fellow diners were a large gray lady in a faded, spotted dress with a pallid, damp sheen on her plain face. Her companion across the table was a stringy middle-aged man with a stained tobacco-tinted face, deeply lined but bright-eyed, wearing an outsized checked shirt that looked almost new.

"Hello," I said. "My name is Graham."

"My name is Enid," the gray lady replied in a broken, staccato stream of words. "And this is Richard. He came in last night. Didn't have a place to stay, or a shirt. I found him a place and a shirt. So what do you think about that?" Without a breath, she continued. "My name is Enid. This is Richard. He came in last night. . . ." She repeated her statement three times allowing no interruption.

As she rattled on, I began asking myself, "What can I say to her? Will she ever stop?" At the fourth rendition, she seemed to slow, so I jumped in.

"Enid," I interrupted. "I think you've just been given a Christmas present," I suggested.

"I've never had a Christmas present in my whole life," she snapped.

"Oh, yes. I think you have," I said slowly. "I think it's Richard."

Richard stopped eating and looked at Enid. Enid looked at Richard, and a small, careful smile began to replace her troubled frown. "Yes," she said, now smiling broadly. "I've got me a Christmas present."

Richard was now pounding his fork on the table calling out, "I'm a Christmas present. I'm a Christmas present."

I was overwhelmed by a totally unexpected joy. I had been out of my depth, and yet I had somehow connected — and, as a result, was rewarded more than I can ever remember at any time in my reward-strewn life.

I left them smiling at each other, and I was smiling too. I had had time on my hands, and it had been well spent.

This story has always moved me because of the simplicity of the people, the dawning of an idea that pleased them both. Just imagine the self-worth felt by both Richard and Enid when Richard said, "I'm a Christmas present, I'm a Christmas present." To me, this is the real meaning of Christmas giving. I love this story. It's almost a parable.

The really neat thing about time is that it can be so personal, so connected with people. Usually, the only thing that holds us back from spending more of it on troubled people is our fear of the unknown. What do I say? What do I do? What if they want more than I have to give?

If we listen to our fears, we will swiftly return to the media maze, vainly using the TV remote to try to find our way to the exit marked "peace."

Imagine with us, just for a moment, what your life would be like if you "tithed" your screen time — the total time you spend each week, during your nonworking waking hours, in front of a computer or television. One estimate comes out at three hours (thirty hours of screen time in fifty-six hours of nonwork time).

Now, let's imagine you visiting your Rotary or Lions Club or church and saying, "I'd like to invest three hours a week in our community. What do you have for me?" Collectively, my friend, we could change our world.

Chapter Eight:
Slow Down
before Turning

What is around the corner?
Do you want to know?
Are you willing to slow down?
Listen, so you'll know?

Most of our discussion to this point has been to somehow see ourselves being carried along on a clear river of life muddied by a mix of self-interest and commercial intent. Somewhere downstream from this point in our global history, we may turn a sharp corner and find ourselves facing a massive series of waterfalls.

Some people seem to hear the sound of many rushing waters. Others are more intent upon fishing for success, while a few are strenuously paddling upstream, calling out warnings to those who float on by. *"There's some really tough stuff round the bend! Check your life jackets and safety lines and helmets."*

We are not entirely sure if this book is an

explicit warning of rough times ahead. We seem to hear the roar of rushing water, and we have a degree of anticipation of considerable cultural challenges ahead. We do know that we would like to be of some help to those who, like us, are prepared to paddle upstream. We may not appear to cover much ground, but we certainly meet a lot of people as they sweep past us en route to the sharp bend in our future.

Going upstream means a change in direction, a deliberate turning away from the normal progression of modern life, along with the added effort it takes to go against the flow.

You may have noticed that we see ourselves and others like us calling out warnings to be prepared for a "rough ride" and not demanding that they pull a U-turn and follow us. That *must* be *their* choice. We cannot (unless we are absolutely certain) tell others what they *must* do with their lives!

Pulling a U-turn in the commercial river of life may well be a combination of three things. The most obvious is that we will be *observed as quite different,* almost to the point of foolishness. The second is to be prepared to put our culture's marketing messages on mute. Our needs must be met; however, *our wants, to a large extent, may be set aside.* The third is to seek out the back eddies of the river where, for small patches, the river reverses itself and allows us to *rest from the ever-present force* of the opposing current in midstream.

You may see here that this kind of change is a mixture of simplification and patience. A great example of this is in the early use of the word *diligence* that comes from the French word *diligère*. *Le Diligère* was used as the trade name of a famous seventeenth-century coach that left on Monday at mid-day and always arrived at its destination, a journey of hundreds of miles over rutted roads, at noon on Saturday. It achieved this remarkable record because the operators chose never to exceed six passengers. They never took more than fifty kilos of freight/ baggage. They changed horses at evenly spaced stops, and as a result, they were always on time. You could rely upon them. They did what they could do and never exceeded that known effort.

In other words, they lived *diligently* or, even more to the point for our discussion, they refused to go beyond *diligence*. Diligence demands a *careful* estimate of our ability, what kind of a load we can carry, for what duration, and for what purpose.

Sometimes, when we are driving through

an especially interesting area, Treena will say, "Why do you have to drive so fast? Can't you slow down? I'd like to see this!" My reply is almost always the same. "I can't. I've already got traffic backed up behind me." My speed isn't always my choice. I'd love to slow down, but to do so I'd have to pull over and even be forced to stop!

So be it!

Slowing down, pulling a U-turn, paddling upstream, resting in the back eddies allows life to happen at life's pace. And natural life takes place season upon season, with all due diligence.

Now, let's see how this may play out in today's commercial river. Treena and I will be detailing our journey of change in the second part of this book. So, for now, let us simply say that *over the years* we've pulled a 180-degree U-turn, but we did it slowly and on purpose.

Do you remember the *Beverly Hillbillies* on television? In the opening titles, Jed and Granny Clampet and the whole family made it to Beverly Hills, Rodeo Drive, in their old truck with everything they valued (and needed?) tied on tight. Now, imagine if they had suddenly pulled a U-turn at about thirty miles an hour. The entire vehicle, Granny included, with all their stuff, would have fallen over on its side. *Smash!*

All of us come complete with both relationships and stuff. Thus we need to slow down, tell everyone to hang on tight, check the rear vision mirror (where we've come from), and then slowly make our turn. In this way, we take care of the things of real value and carry them gratefully into the future.

If we choose to downsize, we may (if we do it with an outdulgent purpose) need less income and, therefore, gain more time. We may be able to pay off a mortgage or a loan and save a lot of interest payments. We may also be able to work fewer hours or at a task that pays less but is much more rewarding.

We can let our "stuff" settle into second place. For more years than I care to admit (yet, we do admit in book 2), I've been employed by my stuff! I had to keep my focus on being a financial success because I had to pay the bills. The bills represented our purchasing the trappings of success — the large house, the large boat, the large cars, the large wardrobes of clothes, the large library of books and CDs. It *all* costs money, and we had to have everything maintained or fixed by someone else because we couldn't *afford* the time to do it ourselves. We had to pay the bills!

The only way to stop doing so was to

somehow "stop the world! I want to get off!"
So we did, slowly!

When we left our past behind, we left the stuff that owned us and drove us beyond diligence. When we left our past behind, we took with us all that we needed, the stuff we owned that helped us live diligently.

When once you've pulled a *well-*considered U-turn, it's not easy to reengage with the complex world of slavery to things, but, as you'll find in our life story in book 2, it *is* possible.

CHAPTER NINE:
MAKING THE
COMPASSIONATE CONNECTION

*Compassion should last not just
for the moment,
not just for a day or a year.
But bring us to see the overall picture of the
hopeless with all their fears.
How do you choose, to whom
does your heart call,
so many peoples with hope almost gone.
Whom should you trust?
Which agency's best? Read on,
precious reader, read on, read on.*

So powerful is the muddied river of modern life that we believe that only a more powerful motive for human change than life itself can allow us to achieve *lasting* change.

Let's face it: "Constant change is here to stay." We are slap-bang in the middle of Alvin Toffler's prophetic book, *Future Shock.* Every time we blink, we engage yet another apparent change as we make every effort to sell each other on the next best thing or experience.

Just like the trees that grew above the Haitian village of Gonaives, we, too, have uprooted the constant to make room for the commercial. By its very nature, the commercial *must* continuously change our desires to obtain their promised upgrades.

So, what could be more powerful than life itself?

- *Patriotism?* Men and women have died for their nation.
- *Religion?* How many have died rather than deny their faith?
- *Community?* There are those who defend us against crime and disaster.
- *Service?* Some people give up their lives in service to others in need.

How admirable are those who, after counting the cost, still put their lives on the line because of what they perceived was the common good. Their passion, their compassion, their absolute commitment didn't die with them. It has lasting value to all of us who, when facing change *for our own sake,* choose to lay down that adverse element of lifestyle and give of ourselves to someone else or to a cause that clearly serves the common good.

We sacrifice a part of our life in order to more fully live in the other part. Only a self-less devotion to someone else can help us to sustain such a change — a change where we lose interest in either *projecting* self (as somehow more important) or *protecting* self (as somehow more valuable, or vulnerable?) than those we choose to serve.

You may remember my coffee story from page 29. Well, a few months later, I realized I was spending $30 a month on appearances.

Graham will be telling you about his "appearance" habits; and I thought to myself, I don't have that as a problem, thank goodness! *I like to look clean and smart, which I can from sales and good thrift stores. But as I have said before, things have never meant very much to me. Rings and bracelets were something one may get as gifts or from a store where they sell Timex watches, which incidentally, seem to last forever.*

While reading Graham's comments, I looked down at my nails and thought, I really must get them done somewhere soon; they look awful! *Appearances? I had been spending $30 a month on NAILS! Oh dear! That's $360 a year for NAILS! So much for my smug thoughts.*

I haven't had my nails done since September 2004. And no, it hasn't been easy, not at all.

This is not a legalism for you or even for me. Oh, yes, I have the money I saved in our out-dulgence account. And it was part of a one-time gift that we gave in early December to an American Indian reservation being served by the church we were attending at that time. It started with four children from the church who went to the reservation to play basketball. And now this team has blossomed into two special teams of American Indians and the church children. Now my nails "go" to Africa for three years.

So, who are these people for whom we would be prepared to lay down a portion of our chosen lifestyle? We frequently hear the phrase "through no fault of their own," followed by a serious, sometimes apparently hopeless situation like homelessness and abject poverty. And yet, on closer inspection, sometimes we can see that there was, in fact, some level of personal failure that prompted their experience.

Our first suggestion, therefore, is not to think of those in need as basically a noble people just waiting to burst forth into the sunshine of opportunity and bloom! How disconcerting to find that "they" are really just like us — all too human, too ready to exploit generosity, and occasionally prepared to reject the very people who helped them. By no means are these reactions the rule, but as exceptions they often so disappoint the donor that compassion dissipates, and indifference sets in. Exactly why people are in hopeless situations shouldn't be our focus. Rather, our minds should search out a solution, a way to break them out of their cycle of despair.

Over the past thirty years, we have had the opportunity to see much success (and, yes, also failure) for some people to find freedom and purpose through personal faith, which we will be discussing in detail in the second part of this book.

Because book 1 is dealing more with facts and human logic, let's explore some practical aspects of this daunting issue.

Clearly we are surrounded by human needs. The sheer volume of need is overwhelming: for example, the twelve million children under five who died last year from malnutrition-assisted disease.

His eyes go from the polished bowl
Of steaming rice to daughter's face.
Her large brown eyes, gentle, knowing,
Tear at his resolve, for she lies dying
In the arms of one who bore this child —
His only girl child in whom he so delights.

Yet eat he must to give him strength,
To work to feed his boys and wife.
His father heart now breaks with anguish,
As gnarled and shaking fingers
Slowly bring the rice up to his lips.
Her eyes, they never leave his face.
She smiles. He eats.
To quench his thirst? His tears.
They will forever be his drink.

The deeper we choose to dig, the more intractable the problem appears to be. During our search for someone we might help, we wondered about that word *compassion* and why it seemed different from *sympathy, empathy, social justice, social activist, mover and shaker, world-changer.* We began to see that the word, used in its active-reaching-out-to-fix-something meaning, derives from the Greek word *splagchnizomai* — quite literally "to be moved with, or to have compassion." It was apparently something we felt inwardly, not necessarily with our "mind" or "heart" but rather in the "spleen," which, by the way, is taken from the first part of *splagchn-(izomai).*

So, compassion should help to guide us to select our part in the overall picture of bringing hope to the hopeless.

We began by using the first seven letters

in *compassion,* or *compass.* A compass is always used to find one's way, so it seemed highly appropriate.

All compasses comprise 360 degrees and are divided into 45-degree segments, such as north northwest (NNW) and south southeast (SSE) — a total of eight pie-shaped pieces. We divided our compass into eight servings of hopelessness.

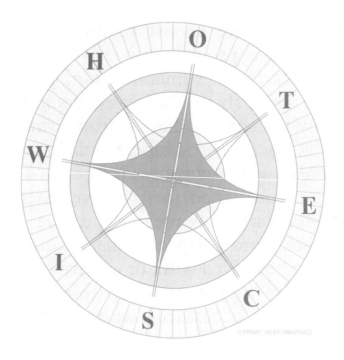

1. **H**unger
2. **T**hirst
3. **C**lothing
4. **"E**xiled" from home-based relationships (refugee, etc.)

5. **S**ick
6. **I**mprisoned/persecuted
7. **W**idowed (without family help)
8. **O**rphaned (without either parent)

I'm sure that we could easily subdivide each of these slices into tiny slivers of specific need until we would be faced with at least 360 degrees of issues "demanding" compassionate attention. But, then we'd be back into the complexity of searching for a single need, one with which we could truly *connect*.

So, we focused upon our basic megalist and began our search for which of the eight (one or perhaps more) really went beyond sympathy or empathy or even our outrage at injustice, into that strange action-compelling sense of compassion.

Please revisit that list with us and see if one (or perhaps two?) appear to cause you some inner desire to help somehow. We found it easier to remind ourselves that the recipients would all be seeing their situations as *hopeless,* and that only with our participation might they begin to receive hope.

Hungry
Thirsty
Clothing

Exiled
Sick
Imprisoned
Widow
Orphan

We have compiled a list of agencies, typically known as NGOs (non-government organizations) who serve those in these "hopeless" situations and who may be your way of connecting with those in greatest need of your compassion. This list is in appendix A, which begins on page 331. We urge you to scan those opportunities under the segment to which you feel compassionately drawn.*

All too often, at this point in the search, we find ourselves distracted by the next best thing or some urgent problem that needs to be fixed, like the massive Indian Ocean Tsunami disaster. In the distraction we may lose that fragile, threadlike connection that can lead us into truly life-changing experiences accompanied by great joy and lasting satisfaction.

We have so many good intentions: "Yes, this

*The list is not meant to be exhaustive, only to provide a range of *real* opportunities to help you define *your* direction.

I will do — maybe next week." When next week passes, and the next and the next, the good intention has all but turned to nothing. Maybe one's husband doesn't agree, or other important things take up one's time. Or we allow our time to be frittered away on a shopping spree with girlfriends, a lunch, tennis, golf. All those caring thoughts swiftly turn to dust and blow away. There's just no time. It's so much trouble to find a good agency. Then on another day a different speaker, preacher, or missionary sweeps away the dust and reveals within our hearts the seed of good intention waiting to be born again! Or blown away?

So, *please* take the time to narrow the field and make that inquiry and begin to question several agencies about exactly what they do, where they do it, and, most important (for you), to whom they minister.

You likely will find, as we did, that compassion is most effectively felt for another human being or family and perhaps less effectively (in the long term) for a cause or even a community.

This is, however, *your* search, and we passionately believe that there is someone, somewhere who will be somehow set free by your outdulgence. As you recover your abundant good health, so will they begin to glimpse hope.

As you now begin your search, just a word of advice. You, like ourselves, may be justifiably concerned that the agency to whom you send your money will somehow misuse it so that little actually gets through to the object of your compassion. We have all seen the media horror stories of both misuse and downright theft of charitable money, but this, thankfully, is *not* the norm. Nonetheless, you should inquire of those agencies what their administrative and fund-raising overheads are as a percentage of overall receipts.

Contrary to immediate logic, the lower percentages of overhead are not necessarily the best. We know of some NGOs that are almost ruthless in their elimination of overhead. Unfortunately, the environment in which those agency workers have to operate is sometimes almost savage in its austerity, and many good-hearted folk are exploited to the degree that they cannot give their best effort. And, notwithstanding the monetary aspect of the original gift, the love that should be there at its distribution is missing!

Sometimes infrastructure can be as important as the service itself. In the case of hunger, for example, an agency may provide tons of food for those starving, yet that food is worthless unless there is a delivery system for getting it into the hands of the people in need. And trucks and helicopters cost money too.

Over the years, we have found a balance in our searches and believe that all overhead, including *all* fund-raising efforts, should not exceed 25 percent of gross receipts. This may not be the case for relatively new agencies, but it should certainly be possible for those that are well established.

Questions to ask NGOs

Dear [Try to find a *real* person to address!]

We are about to commit a part of our present lifestyle to help serve others in need. We want to make a three-year commitment to reach [insert the category of your compassion; i.e., "the hungry in Africa"].

Because of the length of the commitment, we obviously want to make the wisest possible choice. Would you please help us to do this by answering the following questions:

1. How would you best describe your overall vision to reach the needy?
2. We are especially interested in [insert "need" here]. Please share where and how you help these people.
3. Can you openly share personal faith when you meet needs?
4. Where, if any, do you encounter resistance to share personal faith? Please explain, if possible.
5. Are your services mostly relief or long-range development?
6. How do you raise the majority of

your financial support?

7. As a percentage of your gross receipts, how much do you devote to . . .
   - fund-raising?
   - education at point of need?
   - delivery systems to point of need?
   - raw materials?
   - specific administrative overhead?

8. Does any accountability/review organization report publicly on your works? If so, who?

Thank you for your help. If you could include recent newsletters, and so forth, that report upon your hands-on ministry, we'd be grateful.

With Sincerity, [or your sign-off]

Our next proposal may well appear to be too big to jump, and so we literally submit it for your *careful* consideration. We do not even suggest that it be an absolute, even though, after many years, it has become so in our lives.

The word *careful* has now been used *twelve times* in only eight chapters. So it must be pretty obvious that we mean it! Let's look at the word *care* before we come to the big hurdle because without its meaning it is entirely possible to knock the hurdle flat on its side.

To care — a definition using an acronym:

C. Concern
A. Altruism
R. Restoration
E. Enthusiasm

We used the dictionary to define each word.

Concern: to have one's mind filled with . . .
Altruism: a selfless devotion for the well-being of another
Restoration: to return something to its original design intent
Enthusiasm: root *en-theos* (Gk), meaning "in God"

110

So to care, using the above explanation, is: "To have one's mind filled with a selfless devotion for the well-being of another so that they may be returned to their original design intention in God."

Now, armed with this definition, let us *carefully* examine the "Three-Year Commitment."

CHAPTER TEN:
THE THREE-YEAR LEAP

*It takes at least three years for a seed
to grow and flourish all on its own.
Thus also a human from hopeless to hope
may need more to make hope their own.
We should make sure we give no less than
three years of compassion and folded self.
This money released by change you've made
will bring healing to them both and yourself.*

Making a contribution to another's life so
that they can find genuine hope is not unlike growing a vegetable garden from scratch
in untilled, virgin soil. It takes three years
to begin to see a vibrant, natural organic
garden flourish. It can easily take more than
three years to provide a "real" hope to the
hopeless, but three is an excellent beginning.

We have also found, again from years of
experience, that it takes three years to let an
old, harmful habit gradually fall into disuse,

112

literally unable to regain our attention and once again dominate our choices.

It is really funny that a bad habit takes no effort to become part of one's life, but to develop a good habit takes a great deal of effort. It's easier to be critical than positive; easier to see weeds than to notice flowers; to look up and see the cobwebs rather than the sky; to notice what needs to be done than what has been done. These are bad habits that are hard to break. I know them all. I also know that, given time, these too will pass.

So, for both sides of the outdulgence issue, we find that a three-year commitment *is* a good place to start!

To help you wrestle with this idea, we offer some other points to consider. The first is that donors appear to suffer a great deal from what we call "fickle funding." By this we mean our tendency to "flit from flower to flower" — to commit to give for a season and then to switch to the next best offer to serve the hopeless.

The problem lies in the highly understandable fact that many agencies that started a good work began to rely upon a certain volume of charitable contributions to back their commitments to serve people. Where several other agencies sprang up performing more or less exactly the same service, there was a predictable reduction in funds received all round.

Because the first agency was experiencing a shortage in cash flow, they felt compelled (because of their commitment and compassionate connection to human need) to make a more impassioned plea for funds. And so, today, we have layers upon layers of well-meaning folk bringing more or less the same set of services to the hopeless.

Surely that's good, right? Well, not necessarily! As regular donors, we are often asked by either new or "competitive" agencies to give to their cause. We've noticed that the way in which the requests are phrased seems to be getting more and more manipulative and, therefore (for us), easier to reject — even, in some cases, without opening the envelope!

This is how we have reached a kind of "compassion saturation," where we get more experience saying no than yes.

A stranger leaned on the garden gate,
Where a "sweetheart" lady, with silver hair,
tended her flowers with loving care.
Seeing the stranger, she smiled a sad smile,
"I'm lonely, you know,
though it has been awhile

since my Archie died on a Saturday morning.
It happened so quickly, without any warning!
Won't you come in?
I could give you some tea,
but perhaps you've not time to visit with me.
The stranger said quietly, "I've no other call!"
"I do miss his laughter,
sounds from his footfalls,
which echoed throughout
these long corridors.
The silence is awful, so empty with gloom.
What would you do with these
cold empty rooms?"
"I'd find someone who had no place to stay:
A pregnant child, or a scared runaway.
I'd look for a person who was truly deserving,
A soul, whose existence you'd feel
worth preserving.
Your house would then
have life in these rooms,
your corridors echo with footsteps,
not gloom.
Their love would embrace
your spirit with song —
no longer lonely, your heart would belong.
"NO, it would not. What a horrid idea!
My home would be ransacked.
Me, full of fear!
NO. Not only that, what
would my friends say?

They'd think I'd gone crazy
and stay far away!"

The joy — had she said YES —
to God's needy ones,
The pleasure to all, if compassion had won.
Both witnessing peoples and
angels would stare
At her selfless love; but it just wasn't there!
Had she trusted her friends,
showed them the way,
Had she brought to her home
just one runaway,
Perhaps the stranger may
have waited to share:
He was one of those angels,
received unaware!

When too many say no to their annual campaigns, you'll find agencies asking desperate questions and facing truly awful decisions: "Do we try this 'new' method, or do we stop or scale back our promises to the hopeless?"

This is why we are so keen on the three-year commitment:

- It forces us to do our initial home-work diligently (or carefully!). When we know it's for three years, we will be much less likely to give impulsively and, therefore, less likely to change at the prompting of another sudden whim.

- We want to know about ongoing progress and plans and, therefore, tend to hold the agency more accountable for their future actions.
- The habit we've converted to cash has a nice long time to die out completely!
- The agency will be able to plan ahead, being more confident in the longer-term commitment.

By the way, when we make our commitment, we promise to give the agency a one-year notice of change, i.e., at the end of year two, we may give a detailed reason why we are deciding to make a change. This is a valuable tool because it can be used to continuously shape the services to meet *present* needs and not let things simply settle into comfortable, conservative, possibly less-effective ruts. As a service to you, we've included a draft letter of commitment to an agency for you to modify to suit your own needs. You will find this as appendix B on page 341.

Chapter Eleven:
The Investment Process

*Whether done in a group or family or just
by a single cowboy,
Open an outdulgence savings account,
to give to a poor girl or boy.
The decision is yours and yours alone.
There's no "must" or "ought to"
to bring shame.
However, to us, it feels better
than any great fortune or fame.*

It's now time to actually "bite the bullet" and discuss how we might convert all this logic into what the British call "lolly." I only mention this because I'm obviously attracted to alliteration, and turning logic into lolly only works if you understand the word!

So, logic becomes money, and money is what Treena and I call "folded self." The way we see it (because we inherited no money from either set of parents) is that the money we now have and will receive has been earned by selling people our time and receiving payment for those hours spent.

Because time is an absolute measure of outflow, it really does represent our life — or self! Thus "folded" money is a mark of those transactions, which is why we call it folded self. We have, we hope, spent enough of *your* time for you to agree with us that there are a great many ways for us to exchange our "folded self" for goods and services. What we need to do is somehow make sure that our desire to give isn't absorbed by the next best thing.

We chose (eventually) to set up a special account at our bank that we call the outdulgence account and to issue instructions to the bank to transfer, on the first day of each month, the accumulated total of our lifestyle decisions to date along with any special, one-time decisions we may have made during the preceding month. We then have an amount that is designated to be given *creatively* to the hopeless and can be distributed again by the bank using electronic fund transfer services (EFTS).

We are really committed to the idea of carefully assessing our actual savings, and we know that this may not be your style. You may actually dislike the "bean counting" process, while at the same time really enjoying the way you currently respond to those in need.

Sometimes our lifestyle changes are personal — like mine from the coffee and my nails. The savings go directly into our joint out-dulgence account. Now we always agree on every project we support; however, I'm given my very own people to be helped, so I can fully connect the habit change to an actual need. I need that unbridled feeling, and it works nicely in our marriage.

Obviously, we don't want to use the word *must* or to introduce "rules." What out-dulgence is all about is sequence. It's not a "system." Therefore, all we can ask is that you observe, from our own journey, what appears to work *in the long term.* We know *exactly* what we saved when we went from *threat* levels of consumption to *treat*-sized portions, and, therefore, we have a way to measure the moderation that many hold up as an ideal but few can describe accurately!

The dollars we spend from day to day on a consistent basis are called disposable income. It's the cash left over after a big-ticket mortgage, loans, and so forth; and it's these amounts, when released, that keep our economy dynamic. What we purchase on an ongoing, consistent basis (disposable dollars) are lifestyle choices that either provide quality and both emotional and physical health, or accumulate to rob us little by little of what matters most — our overall sense of wellness.

WHAT ARE THE FEELINGS OF WELLNESS?
It's a glowing inside of blessings and love,
A shimmering source of pure joy to apply,
Or a dance in the breeze like a butterfly.
One knows one could live as a
queen or beggar,
Sing a song full of praise and thanksgiving
As gratitude pours from
one's innermost being
Because of that glorious, glory-filled feeling.

Many of our illnesses come from our choices, and that's why science often suggests that we consume less of some choices and more of others. When we work out the actual cash difference in these choices, it is almost always true that we see a small savings.

What is so neat about *small* savings is that they add up (if we take the time to do the simple math). For example, we reduced our cookie intake to four a day. It saved us only 68¢, but that adds up to $248 a year. And that, over a three-year basis, is $744 (or in the six years since we've started: $1,488). Because we kept the record, we have a real story to tell — one that can be measured. That's why, whether it happens to be your style or not, it's a very valuable use of your time!

Graham and I really do have a partnership in purpose. It isn't just his ideas; we talk everything over together. And it can be such fun when, regardless of our different styles, we still turn out to be compatible. Never forget that your own personal savings in your own personal style make you a full partner!

Our PSI (personal sphere of influence) is the good we can do with our lifestyle choices. We can also link up with others to increase our impact.

Imagine, if you will, a small pond in a wooded area. You take a stone and throw it in. There's a splash, and ripples rush across the surface. Drop to your knees and see what those ripples do to just a few inches of the muddy edge. A leaf may shift, some earth may dissolve slightly, and then the surface is still again. In some minute fashion, everything on the pond's rim where the water meets the earth has been changed.

That's *our* PSI — our small pond for just a moment in time — and we *know* that we made a difference.

Now, take the same sized stone and throw it into a lake. It's hard to see what impact you made, if any, unless you are Bill and Melinda Gates. This is why we like the idea of combining our small contributions with others of like mind. It's amazing what a difference we can make.

The idea of outdulgence can be used by a group of any kind — Rotary, Lions, a church, a community, or even a business can be invited to assess individual lifestyle choices and contribute their savings to a specific task that needs a little bit more cash flow to be successful. For this to work, there has to be a *true* consensus within the group. Somehow, the group must *own* the way in which the hopeless are being reached. This will *not* happen overnight and, regardless of the apparent drama associated with the need, it shouldn't! Dramatic needs usually mean immediate relief is called for, as in floods, earthquakes, and some famine situations. This should be a clear-cut, one-time response.

The cure for hopelessness is often a matter of consistency in the services provided — the very reason why we are so fond of the three-year commitment. Getting a group of people to commit to three years isn't easy, but, nonetheless, the outcome can be immensely rewarding for everyone concerned.

We have found that it works best when the whole group embraces the connection between possible harmful habits and the world of needs out there. We invited our first group to begin contributing their lifestyle choices (at least fifty cents per person per day) to a single savings account. (We had one recorder who issued receipts for tax purposes.) We then met to consider how we could make a *lasting* commitment, and to whom, with what was accumulating. That was nearly twenty years ago, and some of us are still giving to the same development project that we selected in the Amazon.

Whichever way you choose to engage with the idea, it is our greatest wish that you would experience joy through a real sense of personal achievement.

If I may press the point once more, we must own the compassionate feeling for those to whom we are giving. If we don't, my friends, we will lack the essential desire to be consistent and will use our savings to buy the next best thing. How sad when promised money no longer comes. The sadness is so deep, we ourselves may feel a sense of loss.

You may find that this lifestyle change gives you the strength to drop a persistent habit that you've never been able to change, no matter how hard you tried. The difference is that you have linked your decision with the needs of another whose very life hangs in the balance. You may find healing, and our world becomes — albeit microscopically — a better place, and you become a witness to a miracle.

And now, since we have arrived at the miraculous, it seems like a good place to see how all this logic worked out in a practical, measurable, yet miraculous manner in our own lives.

Book Two:
Our Thread of
Faith Passes
Through the
Eye of Our
Lifestyle

Book 2
Introduction

There is always a beginning to every change and thus it is so with us.
We sincerely hope this will help you set out on adventures you'll share with us.

Treena and I came out of our cardiologist's office positively glowing.

"Well done!" I hugged her and bussed her cheek; her smile was too broad to kiss!

We had a great report. Treena's cholesterol was way down; her blood pressure was fine. Her stress test showed that she was 40 percent fitter than the average woman her age who *hadn't* had a heart attack, stroke, or hypertension.

I wanted to know if we could celebrate by sailing our thirty-six-foot sailboat from Anacortes in the San Juan Islands to Glacier Bay in Alaska — a twenty-four-hundred-mile round trip, just the two of us.

Dr. Landreth reviewed his report one

more time, closed it carefully, looked me in the eye as only a physician that runs ten miles a day can do, and said, "Yes, I believe you can. You've certainly earned the right to take whatever risks there are."

That was 1994, and we had won our lives back and would set out on a grand adventure that we'd worked so hard over many years to achieve. Our route would often take us well beyond cell phone range and available hospitals. We would have several lee shore ocean crossings; we would sail up icebound inlets and anchor off active glaciers. Not bad for a stroke and heart patient!

Treena, as always, kept a detailed log over every mile we covered, as she had done in our previous twenty-four-thousand-mile voyages — every course change, all the weather conditions, all the fueling stops . . . *everything.*

Gosh, do I remember that lo-o-o-ong world trip. I had to do something to keep my mind off the sailing besides watching the mizzen sail (that's the small sail at the back of our seventy-one-foot ketch). I was scared when it tipped, scared in rough waters, scared when our two-year-old, Kareena, would jump off the ship to swim (when we were anchored, of course). So the log was my safety line and kept my mind off the other dramas. The log was full of every-thing — how much fuel we needed, how much water we had, how many nautical miles we had done, how many knots we were going, and, of course, my tears! It gave me a certain comfort as I added my private and personal thoughts. I wrote down every little moan, fear, and the de-tails of every day. The log makes for interesting reading! In 1991, we, or rather Graham, bought another much smaller sailboat, a thirty-six-footer, which we named Dovetail. *This time, I added prayers and "thank-yous" to our log. Now that sailing is over, this log also makes interesting reading. So many of my wimpy prayers were answered. I even prayed God would give us an angel to sit on the anchor and watch over it when we picked it up and laid it out. We are both still here, so obviously that was among those prayers that worked.*

This was not the work of an obsessive/compulsive person. Treena is far from being obsessed with anything. She kept the log because we needed to know where we were at all times in case of a snap fog or emergency (we had no GPS). We relied upon what is called "dead reckoning" to keep us off the rocks. We made it and only glanced off one rock in the whole round trip that took four months. And we had a detailed record that told us (and others) exactly what it was like, in the exact sequence in which it all happened.

This is *exactly* how we've set about writing book 2 of *Recipe for Life*. It's as close to actual happenings as possible since we all have slightly different ways of "seeing" important events. Our journey so far has been a much greater adventure than we could ever have expected when we set out. Please come along with us. Our greatest hope is that it may help you to set out on your own.

CHAPTER TWELVE:
THE WITNESSES

*To tell the truth, the whole truth,
and nothing but the truth, so help us God.
This part of our book is stranger than fiction.
Nevertheless, it's fact and the truth.*

I was once called as a witness in an arbitration hearing in a highly combative situation. It was an extremely uncomfortable experience in which nobody won.

Witnesses obviously want to do the best they can to tell "the truth, the whole truth, and nothing but the truth, so help me God." (Yes, God is still allowed in *that* preamble, probably because money is at stake and not only politics.)

I'm a Christian — we are a Christian couple. All our children have made the same decision since Treena's lead on December 17, 1974. The way we see it is that we are all called as witnesses to the life, times, works, and words of Jesus Christ of Nazareth, both in AD 30–33 and in our individual lives on a day-by-day basis.

Here is the reason we believe this "calling" is true for all Christians throughout the world, no matter what their circumstances may be: "You shall receive power when the Holy Spirit has come upon you; and you shall be My witnesses both in Jerusalem, and in all Judea and Samaria, and even to the remotest part of the earth" (Acts 1:8).

It is because of this verse that book 2 is really all about Jesus. It was Jesus who began the multigenerational "good news" relay race that, more than one hundred generations later, we are still actively passing along as the "witness baton," one to another.

Sometimes, looking back over the past thirty-odd years, I'm embarrassed to say that my witness has been more about me than what Jesus had done and is doing in my life. I know this had something to do with the way we view "celebrity" in the United States. Our early years (1975–78) as Christians were somewhat "frothy" opportunities to present our testimonies to large, enthusiastic congregations. We were recent "converts," fairly well-known "celebrities," and, therefore, newsworthy to some Christians. Our circuit was really quite worldly. It was almost the same media merry-go-round;

only the music was *really* different!

In Treena's case, everything was different. Treena was the focal point of a miracle. God sovereignly reached into our messy, violently unhappy lives and healed her. Treena needed and needs absolutely no convincing that this same Jesus who lived and died two thousand years ago is very much "alive" today. I honestly don't think she noticed the merry-go-round, so sincere and radical was her witnessing.

Some of you have found out how wonderful it is to know you are loved by the Holy Jesus. He did so many new things in my life and most of them seemingly overnight. At first, He took the large rocks of sin from my life, leaving the grit for me to overcome later with His help. I was free and loved and wanted everyone to love Jesus too. How wonderful were those days, weeks, and months. Putting my feet where angels feared to tread (most of the time!), Christian people were so kind and tolerant. I was fearless because I didn't know any better, I suppose. I still am to a certain degree, but now in the Holy Spirit's leading I trust!

As I hope you've noticed, Treena is a poet. She always lets her deepest feelings spill out on paper. For her, words are like the music you get listening to a mountain stream gurgling round smooth stones. Her words are not knit together in a systematic way. They have a rhythm of their own, and they come in a sequence, like a breath-matching heartbeat. Here is her witness to the reality of Jesus Christ:

DECEMBER 17TH 1974
I went to Bethlehem to find
Solace for my tortured mind.
With trepidation as a child,
I lingered with bewildered mind.
A pastor tall and dark did walk the aisle
To greet me with a loving smile.
"My name is Pastor Friend," he said,
A prayer for my unwary soul.
Another extolled, "The angels will rejoice
With Christ and me this very night."
As the congregation prayed
I fell surprised upon my knees —
Then wrenched from deep within my shame
A cry of hope was born within a flame.
"Forgive me, Jesus," cried my heart.
Repentant tears of sorrow filled my eyes,
Burning tears began to fall
Then turned into a waterfall.
Friends, Ruthie and Michelle,
And daughter Tessa too,
Watched and waited silently.

As I stepped — dressed in
Ruthie's gown of white —
Into the concrete bath of blue
Filled with ice-cold water too.
Thus baptized, cleansed from sins,
Although I didn't realize how or why,
A course was set to now live by.
The pastor Chester Friend did ask,
"How would you like to tarry?"
"What is that?" I asked.
"Just waiting on the Holy Ghost."
"Well, might as well as I am here."
I asked, "What do I have to do?"
"Just kneel and thank our Jesus Christ
For the gift He wants to give to you."
Thus I kneeled with eyes tight shut,
Saying, "Thank you" to the name
I had cursed and sworn just hours before.
Suddenly upon closed eyes
A strong light shone, a blinding light.
I opened up my eyes and saw
A Man of brilliance standing there
With joyous smile upon His face.
There upon my heart He placed
His gentle hand; instantly I was filled
With knowledge from within.
I had His Joy, His Peace, His Holy Grace,
And from my living hell, Hope took its place.

I knew nothing of this at the time because I

had been away making TV shows in Canada and returned just in time for Christmas.

The house was beautifully decorated and peaceful. I thought that the unforgiveness we had lived with for more than eight years was simply to be tolerated, but now it was *missing*. Perhaps it was the Christmas effect? Whatever the reason, I was profoundly grateful. Treena was loving, kind to everyone, and her eyes *sparkled!*

I learned about Treena's commitment in a humorous way that has more to do with me than Jesus. So let's fast forward to my offer to join her as a Christian. Her reply was enormously important: "I know that I need Jesus. I'm not sure about you. Why don't you ask Him about that?"

I was free to decide for myself. Treena didn't go to church and made absolutely no attempt to force the baton into my hand.

When I picked up the Bible, one of the first things the Lord seemed to say to me was to put a "golden zipper over my mouth." At least that is how I interpreted it. Later on I read in Psalm 141:3 (NIV) this Scripture, which confirmed what I thought and gave me a prayer to pray back to God: "Set a guard over my mouth, O LORD; Keep watch over the door of my lips." Then I read in 1 Peter 3:1, "Wives, in

138

the same way be submissive to your husbands so that, if any of them do not believe the word, they may be won over without words by the behavior of their wives." So, once again, I had heard, and within three months, Graham came to know and love Jesus along with all our three children, just like the jailer in Acts 16:31.

I watched her with amazement. We had been married twenty years. It's really hard to pull the wool over someone's eyes after all those years.

Treena had changed *overnight.* Yes, she was the same person, and yet she was completely healed of her violent rages and her dependency on multiple prescription drugs. She had gone "cold turkey" on them all and was at peace with herself for the first time that I had known her since we met at school in 1944.

I continued to be amazed and somewhat bewildered because I didn't know how to somehow "connect" with this Jesus who seemed quite unlike the historical religious figure I had heard about in my Anglican public boarding school in England. I could still remember the words to an often-repeated hymn we sang in our school chapel:

"There is a green hill far away,

Without a city wall,
Where the dear Lord was crucified,
Who died to save us all."

Surely that's explicit enough, and I knew those words by heart. I had been "confirmed," but there was nothing personal or life changing. It was all *far away beyond my city walls,* and I had no way of getting there.

It was then that Treena's doctor paid me a visit. "Graham," he said cautiously, "I need to let you know that Treena is completely healed." He paused again, searching for the right words. "I'm a Roman Catholic. We believe in miracles, but I've never seen one that I can't somehow explain with some scientific sequence." He paused again, but this time his eyes filled with tears. "Except this time I can't explain what's happened to Treena. You can't suddenly stop all the medications she was taking without going into a coma, but she did." Now he looked at me closely. He'd moved forward on the couch. "Graham, I believe that God has sovereignly moved into your family and touched Treena. She has received a miracle."

I had been amazed and bewildered, but now I was dumbfounded and no more equipped with a connection. I went into the garden. We had nine acres of lawn behind our 10,800 square feet of home. In the middle of that lawn, among several other trees, we had a huge elm, one of the oldest trees in Maryland.

For the lack of any other contact, I found myself making a one-sided (I'm sure you are relieved to know the tree didn't respond) request of the tree: "OK, I believe God made you and me and Treena. But she's the only one with a living relationship. She's received a miracle, and —" I didn't know what to ask for, so I simply blurted out — "and I'd like a miracle too."

I've come to believe that, no matter how self-serving our felt needs may appear to be, when we cry out to God for a miracle, He hears us and He answers — in His own time and for His own reasons that may take years for us to understand, if ever in this life.

I believe I *now* know exactly what He chose to do, and it was *immediate* and yet completely beyond my understanding at the time.

God simply turned off the lights.

I'm writing this with a silver Mont Blanc mechanical pencil. It was a gift from Treena to celebrate our Silver Wedding Anniversary. I've now written fifteen of my twenty-seven books with it. It has scratches and dents and great sentimental value. But there was a time when it would have "lit up" because it was a treasure and designed to be seen as such. I had surrounded myself with "treasures." Everything I owned had its own "manu-factured light" that had got my attention. I worked really hard, so the rewards needed to match my output. A list isn't necessary. It's really enough to say that *every single light went out!*

It happened immediately after I'd asked the tree for a *miracle en route to a relation-ship.* I had been given what was needed to happen sequentially. My stuff had to be put in the proper balance with who God had always wanted to be in my life. In my case, I couldn't see this light until my lights were either dimmed or extinguished!

I walked back to my "unlit" mansion, past the "unlit" pool and cars, past the "unlit" boats, until I reached my "lit" wife! Over the next thirty days, I stumbled through my suddenly darkened world of stuff, and the only light I could see of any value came from Treena's sparkling eyes.

Imagine everything you own, everything you do, providing absolutely no satisfaction — *none!* I could easily see all that I owned, but the roles had been reversed. They owned me, and gave me nothing in return. I was a slave to my stuff. I worked hard to keep it all going, but it no longer worked for me.

At the end of the thirty days, I literally shouted at the ceiling after a long hard day: "What do I have to say to You to know You like Treena does?" Out of my mouth with the same immediacy as He had extinguished my other lights, He gave me the words that would turn on the identical light He had put in Treena's eyes. I said out loud and without apparent thought, *Jesus, I love You.*

With those words, I became a witness in a case that has yet to be judged, where everyone who chooses to believe wins.

CHAPTER THIRTEEN: SO, WHAT DID JESUS DO OUTDULGENTLY?

He went first, swam upstream,
against the tide of man.
You be next. Go on, try!
Beat that oppressor. You can!

Jesus did everything outdulgently!

And that's our problem: how to select the verses from the Scriptures that completely validate the idea of outdulgence. Any form of extraction would be like offering you vitamin C instead of an orange. A supplement is no substitute for the whole fruit. So how do we explain?

We have lived for many years in or about the Skagit Valley, a lovely saltwater-bordered agricultural valley roughly halfway between Seattle and Vancouver, British Columbia, in Canada. As recently as ten thousand years ago, our valley was more than seven thousand feet deep in ice. As the waters melted and the glacier ice ground down to meet the

Pacific Ocean, there emerged our wide valley and its central river. The Skagit continues to carry melted snow downstream and seven kinds of salmon upstream. At some stage in the opening up of a two-way flow, there had to be a salmon (well, at least two) that decided to go upstream, even though they had not been born in that stream.

Now, please stay with me as I follow them upstream in a brand-new river bordered by few, if any, trees — just barren, muddy silted banks, infertile and in some sense futile, *without abundant life.* Our salmon, "boldly going where no fish had gone before," wind up at the base of a thirty-foot-high waterfall. There is no *natural* instinct to help it to know that it must carry on — only a torrent of water flowing over the top of an impassable barrier.

My choice would be (and has been many times in my life) to simply stop right there. "OK, this is as far as we can go!" I'd say. And so we'd settle, when there was so much more of the river to explore!

Our salmon didn't do that. One of them had to have had an instinct beyond the natural, a will beyond its own to throw itself vertically up that opposing torrent. "Not my will, but thine" (Luke 22:42 KJV).

What now of the second salmon, the one

that witnessed this initial first-time leap? What did that salmon *feel* about making the leap? Whatever it felt, this we do *know:* That it and many, many more — multitudes — have leapt the same leap, season by season, for thousands of years. "If I be lifted up from the earth, [I] will draw all men unto me" (John 12:32 KJV).

Each of those upper reaches of salmon, having given birth to a new shoal of "witnesses," then died, their lifeless bodies fertilizing the barren, muddy banks, creating an enormous fertile bed for today's forests to emerge. "If you want to be My disciples, pick up your cross and follow after Me" (adapted from Matt. 16:24).

Today, some of our Pacific streams no longer offer the same two-way flow. Today there are concrete dams that bar passage, and man-made ladders to somehow help the fish get around the obstacles. Many streams have been stripped of their trees and polluted by agricultural and industrial runoff. "Because lawlessness will multiply, the love of many will grow cold" (Matt. 24:12 HCSB).

We still have wild salmon today in the Skagit River and elsewhere, but everywhere, the commercial needs of man are present and pressing. We pass laws to protect wildlife, especially when a particular species is endangered. "But the one who endures to the end will be saved" (Matt. 10:22 NRSV). Endurance is related to salvation.

I've admitted it; we admit it. It's getting tougher and tougher to follow Jesus upstream. There are so many man-made obstacles that offer us a life without "all that effort" in a comfy, if crowded, fish farm where we can be fed predictably day after day until we are harvested. And then there's the fish ladders that help us negotiate the obstacles and the hatcheries that mimic the gravel beds in the upper reaches. These allow us to think that that's what it means to be born again, causing us to strive just a little on Sunday, yet with a different destination during the week!

Can our streams begin to teem with supernatural vigor once again? Will we throw ourselves upward into the torrent? "All things work together for the good of those who love God: those who are called according to His purpose" (Rom. 8:28 HCSB).

We propose that the idea of outdulgence is captured so well by this triumphant, extraordinary fish, but let's face it; it is only, after all, a metaphor. In Jesus, we go way beyond the metaphor to witness fully man, fully God going all the way upstream to die on purpose, so that we might inherit eternal life. "For you know the grace of our Lord Jesus Christ, that though he was rich, yet for your sakes he became poor, so that you through his poverty might become rich" (2 Cor. 8:9 NIV).

Treena and I are absolutely certain that there is a place "upstream" for us and that we have a God-given instinct for what the *real* place is. It's *not* heaven *yet,* but it's close, and it's in heaven's direction, and the highway (or river) is strewn with choices and opportunities that can lead us from day to day to live an abundant life. Surely this is riches indeed!

But it wasn't always that way.

CHAPTER FOURTEEN:
WHAT IS
ABUNDANT LIFE?

It isn't greed, compromise,
and false appearances,
it isn't fame, affluence, or humongous homes.
It's selflessness, honesty, hearing,
and obeying.
It's forgiveness, repentance, and it's doing
what He's saying.

Let's start off by exploring what it isn't. "Beware, and be on your guard against every form of greed; for not even when one has an abundance does his life consist of his possessions" (Luke 12:15).

If the stream of intent that flows in one's life is about gain, then it will fill the reservoir of the heart with greed. But what is "every form of greed" that I failed for so long to guard against? My wellspring of gain that led to greed came more through *appearances* than envy.

My father's name was John. He and my

mother, Marjorie, were hotel managers, or hoteliers, if you long for the upgrade! This meant that I was raised on a champagne lifestyle with a beer income. We lived on the premises of good to very good hotels. Our rooms were made up daily by servants, our food cooked and served by servants. It was *almost* as if we were to the manor born. And yet, my parents were servants, and I, the only son of servants. My friends were the sons and daughters of customers, customers my parents served. I lived in the company of servants and the upper class, which in England isn't a glass ceiling. It's a steel-reinforced concrete bunker.

There were elements of my life that I liked, but others that I hated, and both won! I liked the attention as the managers' son. I liked to have my bed made and to select my food from a French menu and be served, albeit a little earlier than our customers, but still in the main dining room with its Irish damask tablecloths, silver, and crystal.

I hated to be the son of a servant, to be somehow *less* than my "friends."

My parents had sent me to a private boarding school, at which I had acquired my "southern counties accent" — the ubiquitous BBC announcer voice of that era. I had a few good clothes, but they were *good*. My jacket was Harris tweed; my suit, a country copy of Saville Row. I had a black tie and dinner jacket (tuxedo) so I could attend "hunt balls." My mother would fix my tie and stand back and say, "Oh, darling, you'll knock them dead." I don't think she liked being a servant either. I have no doubt that it cost them dearly to send me to a private school. My parents were not wealthy, and the war had intervened at a time when they might have done a little better.

I was tall for my age and fast on my feet. During my years at "prep" school, I remained unbeaten in the hundred-yard dash; it was my main claim to fame! Then one day a new boy joined the school. He was my age, slightly taller, and, just by looking at him, faster!

At the main sports day that summer, we took our places side-by-side to see who was indeed the faster boy in the school. I got a very good start, and at thirty yards was well ahead (by a few feet!). At the halfway mark, I could hear him coming up behind me. The gap was closing and I was losing. *I couldn't lose.* I strained forward; he continued to gain. In desperation, having nothing else to offer, I deliberately tripped myself and fell headlong onto the track, only a few yards from the finish.

"Oh, bad luck, Kerr," my pals cried out as they helped me to my feet. "You had it in the bag," they encouraged. But I knew better. I didn't want to fail, and my trip had the *appearance* of an accident, and not the *reality* of losing the race.

I have had a hatred for competition from that day on. No matter what the sport or enterprise, I have had a built-in fear of failure largely because of what it would look like to others. *Appearance!* "Let us run with endurance the race that is set before us, fixing our eyes on Jesus, the author and perfecter of faith, who for the joy set before Him endured the cross, despising the shame" (Heb. 12:1–2).

Competition is a brutal taskmaster because it draws a direct comparison with another's efforts. It makes some winners but most losers, and endurance is only possible if we run at our *own* speed and with that to be content. "Make it your ambition to lead a quiet life, . . . and to work with your hands, . . . so that your daily life may win the respect of outsiders and so that you will not be dependent on anybody" (1 Thess. 4:11–12 NIV).

We entered our Christian race a little like an old Volkswagen bug, firing on only three cylinders, entering US 101 at Los Angeles with the highway full of speeding trucks.

We were celebrities, but we were also babies in our faith. All we knew was what Jesus had done in our lives. As we were privileged to meet other Christian leaders, I began to watch what they did and how they spoke. Wanting to win the approval of my new "family," I copied what I liked and did the best I could to avoid what I didn't.

By doing this, I took my eyes off Jesus.

What I succeeded in doing was reproducing what *appeared* to be godly behavior that I now know was an attractive, nonthreatening lifestyle that included good suits, good cars, and attractive, smiling friends. *Appearance!*

One thing I've always tried to do is be *unique.* I was the son of a servant, but I so wanted to be a customer. I was fast on my feet, but I didn't want to be an also-ran. I never ever wanted to be a tourist, always a local.

Being a Christian celebrity seemed to fit this bill quite well. I could still be different and yet be seen as trying to be the same. *Appearance!*

At eighteen years of age, I was called up (drafted) in the British Army as a potential radar mechanic in the Royal Electrical and Mechanical Engineers (REME). At twenty, I was commissioned as a junior officer in the Army Catering Corps. This I didn't especially like. If I'd had my choice, I would have *loved* to be the subaltern that carries the flag at the Queen's birthday celebration in London each year. I knew every move that young officer had to make, and one night when I was in my early thirties, I did the entire parade sequence in the dead of night right there on the famed Horseguards Parade! I was, however, a catering officer in a service not known for its gastronomic pursuit, and, to some extent, I needed to be camouflaged.

I wasn't alone. I had a friend, Haden Jannaway, late of the Irish Fusiliers — a grand, well-educated chap who had been injured and "converted" to the Army Catering Corps. Haden came complete with a set of civilian clothes "to die for." A jaunty, slightly fuzzy bowler hat, a *real* Saville Row suit nipped in at its waist and cut ready to go riding. He had yellow pigskin gloves, a tightly furled umbrella, and an old school tie. Smashing!

So, I did likewise and ran up an impossible bill at *my* tailor (also in Saville Row).

One fine spring day on a weekend pass in London, we were *strolling* as only guard's officers appeared to stroll (really it was an in-step saunter) down past St. James Palace where the Horseguards, the ones with burnished brass breastplates and plumed helmets, stand guard seated on polished, patient horses. As we sauntered closer, we saw the guardsman sizing us up out of the corner of his eye. As we passed, he raised his sword in salute, just in case we were officers that he *should* know. Little did he know (until perhaps now!) that he had saluted two army catering corps officers! *Appearance!* "But those who want to get rich fall into temptation and a snare and many foolish and harmful desires which plunge men into ruin and destruction. For the love of money is a root of all sorts of evil, and some by longing for it have wandered away from the faith and pierced themselves with many a pang" (1 Tim. 6:9–10).

I now possessed the clothes and the accent. I was an officer, and I had learned to saunter. I was well on my way to being known for who I was not.

Oh, my goodness, that bowler hat, that silver-topped cane, and those yellow pigskin gloves. I disliked them ALL intensely and had to get rid of them. I threw the walking stick into the river "Dovey" when we were living in North Wales. The yellow gloves disappeared or wore out eventually. But the bowler hat, Ha! That was a wonderful, delightful, and creative disappear-

ance. I was producing an army show with a cast of the soldiers in the camp where Graham was stationed. Graham was to be "Ertha Kitt's older sister," Earthier Kitt — our surprise guest. I had a blue bed sheet and used it to make him a slinky sarong-type dress. (I needed the sheet again; hence, the sarong.) The dress had a split at the side for his hairy leg. I then purchased a long, black cigarette holder plus cigarette; but the wig, now that was more difficult. I had some black horsehair — don't ask me from where; I have no idea. How could I attach the hair and to what? Then came the great and brilliant idea! The bowler hat. Yes, of course! I cut out the top of the bowler, glued the long pieces of black horsehair to it, and "voila," the wig was an absolute fit to my darling's head. Genius, right?

The show and Graham were a wow! I can't repeat the name of the show (it was before we knew the Lord). When Graham eventually went to wear his bowler again, he found, to his surprise, there was a large hole in the top. "Well, darling," I smiled sweetly, "the show had to go on."

Chapter Fifteen:
One Plus One Equals Two Point Three

One husband, one wife,
equals self-sufficiency.
Add Jesus as Savior,
makes an extra point three!

In nuclear fission, one plus one equals more than the sum of the parts by an extra .3, and it's this extra added energy released by splitting the atom that has fundamentally changed our world by introducing the ultimate paranoia of nuclear war or terrorist act.

Another form of one plus one equals only one, and that happened when we married. It took me years to understand that that first step would lead to another level of "spiritual" mathematics where one plus one plus one equals five; but more of that later.

I married my childhood sweetheart, Treena, on September 22, 1955. We were both just twenty-one, and I was hopelessly, wonderfully in love; I had always been so since we first met at school in 1945.

I felt I could take a deep breath once again, as I had when I left home to join a professional theater group in Jersey in the Channel Islands, and when I left for London to do pantomime. I would now be my own person with someone I loved who loved me. Away from all family influences, this meant freedom and adventure, a better life! It was a new life without any plans or thoughts of the future, or any ambition. When interviewed, I have been asked, "What were your plans for the future?" I answered, "I had none." The interviewer was amazed, shaking her head, "NONE?" "Yes, that's right, none." I was to be married. The future never entered my head! I had agreed to give up the theater to marry, so I had no ambition, just to be a beautiful bride. I was, after all, only twenty-one years old. My father's words still ring in my ears as he walked me up the aisle, "I give this marriage six months!" That is now fifty years ago — so much for his prophetic gift.

And so we became one flesh, with the individual gifting of being both sides of parenthood, both mother and father.

At first, we struggled. Life was certainly

not easy on a junior officer's pay, especially since I had to pay off my tailor in Saville Row (". . . foolish and harmful desires which plunge men into ruin and destruction").

Our daughter, Tessa, joined us on our first wedding anniversary in 1956, followed by our son, Andrew, on January 7, 1960, when we lived in New Zealand. And our youngest, Kareena, came quite a bit later on — October 18, 1969, in Australia. We were now a family of five and had already moved eleven times in those fourteen years. This may not have happened if I had not married Treena. She wasn't the prime mover, but she was always *willing*. Had she not been willing . . . well, she was, and so moving has remained an ongoing feature of our lives.

Why was I always willing to move? I am supposed to have Romanian gypsy blood in me. Evidentially, I am related to the queen of the Romany gypsies! Perhaps that's why moving has never, and may never, be a hassle for me. Moving meant new adventures, new environments, new friends, and a new start. Life could always be better. I really never left my friends because I am still in touch with most of them. But where Graham wants to go, there I go. Packing and unpacking is always a bore, but when once done, the adventure begins.

What about the children, you may ask? Graham always came first; the children really had no choice. No, we didn't pray with them because that was before we came to know the Lord. To my chagrin, I am sure it upset our girls; however, I was prepared for wherever Graham wanted to go. You see, when I was young, an English girl was taught that her husband must come first.

Our son, Andrew, has my "adventurous spirit." Poor Janet, his wife, finds it hard to move and leave her friends, and she is also deeply concerned for their two girls. Andy is more like us — "Let's go. It's going to be fun!" They are all missionaries with Youth With A Mission, a great calling for movers!

Since God became my Father, He is first, then Graham, and we always pray before going anywhere! When two fail to agree, then there can be trouble in the future (Amos 3:3). We agree in prayer, then it is fun and safe. That is the way of this woman — even if you don't agree. It certainly has worked for us!

"Strangers and aliens on route to
a better country."
ADAPTED FROM HEB. 11:13–16 NIV

A truly major change took place in 1958 when we left the United Kingdom for New

160

Zealand. It's hard to imagine a greater distance.

My search for success had led us through some unusual opportunities, all culminating in our gaining the responsibility of general managers of the Royal Ascot Hotel that used to be located quite close to the racecourse made famous by *My Fair Lady.* The hotel has now been replaced by condominiums. We took up the reins (so to speak) following my parents' management when they left to open the now world-famous Gravetye Manor near East Grinstead in Sussex.

We were just twenty-four years old, and what we lacked in experience we made up for in very long hours for weeks on end without a single day off. Of course, we were cheap and very willing, and I was thrilled to have such an early start at reaching my ambition to be the managing director of one of the world's most famous hotels — the Dorchester in London.

I had met the managing director and had been enormously impressed. He wore an impeccably tailored black jacket, waistcoat, and striped gray trousers. His tie was gray silk and held in place with a pearl. Oh, and his accent was substantially the same as mine.

"Not even when one has an abundance

does his life consist of his possessions."

Appearance again — not envy or even ambition!

Our managing director was also the owner, and about him we shall say little. He was an extremely hard taskmaster but undeniably brilliant (though badly dressed.) We learned a great deal, but it cost us dearly when we lost our second child at almost term (seven and a half months).

I believe there is always a terrible sense of loss inside a mother who either loses a baby or has it aborted, whether she is a Christian or not.

I remember a friend of ours had lost their baby girl, a child they both wanted desperately. They already had two wonderful boys, but the father had terminal cancer and wanted a girl to keep Tammy company when he went home. The baby lived for only a couple of days. They gave her a name and a simple, touching funeral.

It was the little one's funeral that brought back remembrances of my own lost baby. I hadn't had a funeral for him, and I hadn't given him a name. I was a Christian now, and it upset me deeply. Carol Pope, another dear friend, said, "Why don't you go home and pray to Jesus, ask Him to bring to your mind a name to give your baby boy?" I did. I gave him my own father's name, Jonathon. (The name was a complete surprise!) Now I know he is there with Jesus, and he has a name!

Here is a poem I would like to share with you. I hope it may provide an understanding for the reason why many women feel such a deep loss, especially those who have had abortions. Babies are God's beautiful creations, and He loves them, every one.

CREATION'S LOVE
Not a fetus, but Creative Life.
Cradled deep within a mother's womb
Begins a tiny seed, a being,
A babe, a wonder, a design,
With potential for the future.
Builder, artist, teacher, author,
Or composer for the people's souls.
Thus begins the breath-filled life,
Preordained from world's beginning
Long before the intercourse of man.
This Holy Gift, blessed for mankind,
Develops slowly: Features form.
Fragile personality is wrought.
Then, tender as a butterfly kiss,
A tiny beat, confirms the life within.

Following Treena's miscarriage, I was advised by our doctor to simply "pretend nothing has happened — just go on as you have been. It will help Treena to get over it speedily." I was mute. Treena desperately needed my love, but I buried myself in the job — or perhaps better put, the job continued to bury both of us. I was learning how costly it would be to be devoted to an ambition at the expense of those I loved the most.

When the muddy stream becomes a series of rapids, even the "white water" is tinted a pale brown. How often I used the cliché "I'm doing all this for you and our family." The truth was that *I didn't want to fail,* and I was way beyond diligence and had no fallback position.

We finally took a partial day off. It was just before the miscarriage. We left before lunch, saw two movies back to back (relaxation!), and returned to enjoy a quiet sandwich in our rooms over the stables. Treena went upstairs to change. I went over to the hotel to order some smoked salmon sandwiches and some milk.

"Graham, there's a big upset in the dining room." Our receptionist was unusually pale and clearly worried. "You gave Stephen [the headwaiter] the day off, and you were gone, and the chairman of BOAC [British Overseas Airways Corporation] arrived for dinner . . ." She raced on to reach the climax, ". . . and we were very busy, and Mrs. Taylor [the owner's wife] took over the restaurant, and, oh, Mr. Taylor was furious. He wants you the *moment* you get back." Now she just stared at me as you'd look at a man condemned to die.

"Where is he?" I checked my watch. It was 9:30 p.m.

"He's in the dining room with the chairman of BOAC," she replied.

"OK, well ask Chef to make up some smoked salmon sandwiches and send them over to our apartment, please." I took a deep breath and entered the now almost deserted dining room.

They had a corner table on the far left, just four of them. Mr. Taylor had his back to the room. Mrs. Taylor caught sight of me first as I approached. She glared.

"Mr. Taylor, sir, you asked to see me?"

"Where have you been with the head-waiter off?" he demanded. By now he was quite drunk.

I wanted to explain that it was our first day off in weeks, but his flushed face, his wife's glare, and the chairman of BOAC made me opt for a simple apology. "I'm sorry, sir," I offered lamely.

"Well *sorry* isn't good enough. Go and stand over there." He gestured to the main entrance in the far corner. I retreated and passed a message via reception to Treena that I was held up and to go ahead and eat. I'd join her soon. It was about 9:45 p.m. Quite soon after, I heard a brief *clink,* followed by the smash of breaking glass. I hurried over to the table. Taylor had broken his wine glass. He still held a table knife in his hand.

"I tried to get your attention. Now see what you have done?" I cleared away the mess while Mrs. Taylor glared. I returned to my corner. It was 10:00 p.m. Remaining diners had now left; only one waiter and myself remained.

It was 11:00 p.m. when the party rose to leave. "Get the Chairman's Rolls," demanded Taylor. I stood by the entrance to the huge, tree-shaded stable yard as the Rolls Royce crunched over the gravel, its huge Lucas lights cutting a swath through a light ground mist. The chairman emerged, Taylor at his side. "Good night, sir. Good night, madam," I offered quietly as I opened the main doors. They all ignored me. For them, I seemed not to exist.

Then Treena emerged from the night. She was by then more than six months pregnant and wearing her diaphanous housecoat that billowed out behind as she ran barefoot swiftly across the lawn and onto the gravel drive in front of the Rolls, caught for a moment like a giant moth in the headlights. "You _____, _____, _____." She began a long and detailed description of Mr. Taylor's dubious birthright, his racial background, his general behavior. She left little out — and then she fainted.

Why would I do such a thing? Good question. We had not had a day off in sixteen weeks. We had had a lovely day, and I just wanted to end the evening with my Gra and quietly enjoy our little supper. As time went on, one of the staff arrived with a sandwich for me. "Where is Graham?" I asked. "He is with Mr. Taylor; he shouldn't be long." So I waited. I didn't eat the sandwich; I wasn't hungry. I just wanted to spend the time with Graham. I rang the reception and asked my friend, Gwen, at the desk, "What's going on?" She replied, "You really don't want to know." "Yes, I do!" So she told me the story and explained that Graham had said he would be back very soon and would tell me the rest when he saw me.

Another hour went by.

I was now furious with Mr. Taylor and the injustice of everything. So I flung on my dressing gown and stormed down the steps into the courtyard, just as Mr. and Mrs. Taylor came to the back door of the hotel with another man and Graham trailing behind them. I had intended to confront Taylor in the dining room, but now I could encounter him face-to-face. I vented all my pent-up feelings and fainted on the spot.

"Good night, sir. Good night, madam," I repeated with much the same calm as before. I moved forward, bent down, lifted Treena up with a certain amount of effort, and strode off into the night. It seemed as if *they* no longer existed.

It was 11:15 and my career path had changed; we were about to experience a beer lifestyle on a little less than a beer income.

The Taylors chose to say nothing, even though Mrs. Taylor continued to glare.

Treena chose to ignore Taylor completely; for her he had literally ceased to exist.

I began to look for another job that might even remotely be back on track for the Dorchester.

Our baby's heart stopped beating.

Treena's heart was broken.

I kept on trying to stay on track.

Now, while the next six years would be lots of fun to write about, they lend little to how outdulgence came to be. In fact, they were filled with the exact opposite. I never got to wear a Saville Row suit with striped pants and a gray silk tie. I was never able to greet the rich and famous at the Dorchester. "Good morning, my Lord . . . your Highness . . . your Majesty," etc., etc.

We did, however, pull up all our roots and escape to New Zealand, where we began our lives all over again. Andrew joined us when we were twenty-six, before we had saved enough to afford a car.

Treena worked part-time at a milk bar (corner deli) for fifty cents an hour, making unmentionable sandwiches such as baked bean and even potato chips! I walked to work and re-sold vegetables to my fellow officers to augment my marginal income. We survived, and after some tough times, we began to be happy.

Before long, out of the closest we've ever been to real poverty, opportunities began to open — radio, television, Wine and Food Society, books, and Treena's return to the theater.

While Graham was away, I thought I'd go and audition for an acting job in radio. I really didn't want to make bean sandwiches anymore! When Graham returned, I naturally told him what a thrill it was to come away with the lead for the following week's broadcast play. I was so excited I asked him to listen to the play with me. It was terrible!

I realized I was doing the part as though I was back on stage. My voice was flat, and I needed to act with my voice. My actor friends and producers helped me through the parts in the other plays I was given. Oh, it was such fun to be back acting again, and I brought in some money. I fell in love with radio and have loved it ever since.

What did Graham say? "That's great, darling. It's not the theater; the actors are different." Little did he know that most of the actors in radio were professional theater actors from England. At that time, there was no professional theater in New Zealand.

It was then that our greatest trial began to show up on the western horizon. Australia beckoned and I responded. Television shows were made, not unlike our early efforts on New Zealand's brand-new, solitary television network, where I was paid twenty-five New Zealand pounds an episode for a show that played nationally between *Peyton Place* and *The Avengers* at 8:00 p.m.!

In Australia, it was more. We actually got four hundred Australian pounds a show, which seemed like an absolute fortune following our five years of hand-to-mouth existence.

CHAPTER SIXTEEN:
SEDUCED
BY A SUITCASE

Seduction is subtle, leads one to fall.
Before one knows, it brings sadness to all.
Trust is now lacking, innocence fled.
To forgive is not easy although it is said!

Our initial budget in Australia was slim, so I had to travel alone, make shows quickly, and hotfoot it back to our simple, low-cost apartment overlooking Wellington's busy downtown and dock area. I made an initial thirteen episodes in about a week, heaved a sigh of relief that it was over, pocketed more than five thousand Australian pounds *(for only one week's work!)*, and put Australia behind me. I simply couldn't imagine the program being a success in such a sophisticated environment.

My brand-new manager almost shouted down the phone, "Get back over here NOW! You're a hit! So OK, move it — we'll do another twenty-six." He was plainly taking a lot for granted. When I seemed to resist, he quickly increased the price I would get per episode. It is said that every man has his price, and within a minute or so I had discovered mine. The four hundred pounds Australian had seemed a fortune. What I would now receive was beyond reason.

I packed my clothes, scooped up twenty-six program outlines I'd already done in New Zealand, and tightened the leather strap around my composite-fiber, green suitcase. The case had seen many years, but it kept my clothes dry, and the strap allowed an extra measure of security that the clasps and hinges no longer provided. I got a warm send-off from Treena, and then I was on my way into the storm.

My first jolt came going through customs. What looked like a very senior customs officer, with lots of gold braid, made a beeline for my bag. "Is this yours?" he asked.

"Er, y-yes," I stammered, "but I've got nothing to declare." I've always felt somewhat anxious in the company of uniformed officials.

"Oh, all I want to do is put my initials on your case." He grinned and made a chalk mark on a part of the green fiber less scuffed than the rest.

"Why?" I asked.

"I'm a fan. I watch your show all the time." He pounded me on the back for good measure. "Your Rolls Royce limo is outside," he added with what looked like a knowing wink.

I'd taken a taxi in on the last visit. *What was happening?*

The dark clouds gathered.

The driver — or should I say *chauffeur* — took my bag as though it was contaminated. "Is this *yours,* sir?" he asked with borderline sarcasm as he placed it gingerly into the trunk.

As we drove into Sydney, I sat in silence in the back, watching the lights and the crowds as we pulled up at the Chevron Hilton that overlooked Darling Point where the Sydney Opera House juts out into the harbor.

The clouds began to flash with far-off lightning.

I was taken to the Penthouse Suite (notice the capitals). Those were the days of deep shag carpet. In this case, you needed snowshoes to get about. I tipped the bellman, who had asked, "Do you want *this* on the bed?" By now, I was deeply ashamed of the bag that had served me so well for so many years, and at the same time overwhelmed by all the attention I was getting. *Talk about an upgrade!*

One wall of the suite was all glass and looked over King's Cross to the harbor. I was confronted by a million lights reflecting off still, dark water, the deep carpet underfoot, the huge soft bed, contrasted with my green, composite-fiber suitcase with its leather strap and recent chalk mark. I just sat there and cried, tears pouring down my face. The lightning flashed and I heard the thunder rolling in. I had entered the storm. I had come too far, too soon, without the usual struggles that accompany success.

To the casual observer, my life had suddenly taken an incredible upturn. In fact, it appeared to go vertical. It was vertical, but there are two directions to vertical — up and down. I was going down rapidly on the inside and climbing up as swiftly on the outside.

This was to be my first encounter with the *reward for effort* lifestyle. Up until this point, Treena and I had worked really hard and just broken even. We'd saved very little, we owned even less, but we were happy. We had time with each other and our friends. We were pretty well who we appeared to be.

And then I exchanged my green, composite-fiber suitcase for a "leather portmanteau." It was the kind of suitcase owned by a very privileged few. The next time porters and chauffeurs held my bag, they'd have a different attitude about who I was. I took my sudden financial windfall and began to wrap myself about with the "stuff" that had a message. Outside Regent's Palace in London, Haden and I had been mistaken for guard's officers. Now perhaps I'd be mistaken for a celebrity!

CHAPTER SEVENTEEN:
GOING VERTICAL

Going vertical is both up and up and down.
The old axiom, out of sight, out of mind.
Fame can bring pride, thus pain to others.
Forgiveness can come, but only through
Jesus.

Going vertical is a breathless experience. Things seemed to flash past at increasing speed. Momentum is the big issue, not so much the effort, because sudden acceleration builds up a special continuum all its own. In the blur, people became less important, possibly because they were quickly left behind. If colors streak and become muted, what about the conscience? On my way up the slippery slope, I pulled up my values and converted them to commercial opportunity and personal reward.

I began to cause pain; others began to suffer.

The momentum continued. I tried to dry

the tears, but the pressure was on. I couldn't get off. The G-force of gratification was pressing me back into my new sophisticated image. *I couldn't move!*

With another series recorded, along with the sponsors' advertising messages, I returned home. I now traveled first class, to match my luggage. Treena met me at the door, radiantly happy at my return. After an embrace, we moved into our little space that she had spring cleaned for my return.

"Oh my, but isn't all this shabby!"

Shabby compared to the Penthouse, perhaps, but that was not what Treena had experienced. I might as well have struck her across the face.

Tears welled up in her lovely eyes. She had no way of understanding because neither did I. We stood there, held together yet miles apart in the eye of the storm.

My darling was coming home. I scrubbed and polished and vacuumed up and down the stairs. In fact, I had spent the whole of the previous day getting ready. I had even made curtains for a large wardrobe and had quilted the ceiling with material and gold studs. This was actually a very small room where at least one person could now stay for the night. I was so thrilled. The house looked lovely.

I welcomed Graham home with such joy, waiting for him to praise our spic-and-span paradise! I couldn't believe his remarks. Perhaps he was joking. But he wasn't. I was devastated.

What was wrong? What had I done? I had worked so hard! I felt as though I had been stabbed in the heart.

Fortunately, it didn't take long for the hillside of my selfishness to subside. I'd pulled up so much that I had valued that there was nothing to hold it back when it became saturated. We were buried, yet somehow we surfaced, and there we remained floundering in the thick mud and debris of pain and unforgiveness.

For eight long years, we were carried along by the momentum of that mudslide. We worked together. We clung to each other, but the pressure of commitment and obligation never gave us the *time* to find ourselves — until the *crash!*

We were on U.S. 101 and had left Santa Barbara en route for San Francisco in a small caravan of recreational vehicles and a trailer as we set out to film our way around the United States for *The Galloping Gourmet* series. We were to make 130 episodes and complete our contract for the 650.

We were somewhat asleep in bunk beds, on either side of the RV. We were being driven by a professional each night as we filmed during each day. We were pulling a sixteen-foot trailer loaded with camera equipment.

Suddenly, we were struck from behind. The truck was reported to be doing about seventy miles an hour. We were poking along at forty to forty-five. Our world stopped, and a whole new momentum took over.

"*All* things work together for the good of those who love God; those who are called according to His purpose" (Rom. 8:28 HCSB). (Even before some of us have the slightest idea what that purpose may be!)

Our trailer was crushed, the last five feet of the RV was destroyed. Treena and I were catapulted from our berths into the saloon area. We were hurt but we were alive.

We had crawled out on the bough of the tree of success — all the way out to the end and the branch had broken! We couldn't climb back up. We tried, but we had nothing left.

Treena was badly traumatized. I was partially paralyzed. We offered our apologies to all those "inconvenienced," but we had had it! We packed up our home, licked our wounds, gathered up our children, and went in search of a long-awaited healing.

■ ■ ■ ■

By this time, early in 1971, we had sacrificed much to the drive for success, or was it the fear of failure? We were together again, or was it for the first time?

Achievement, whether by design or accident, is like a drug. There is always some goal "out there" ahead of the struggles of the day that seems to make the pain worthwhile or at least justified. So, what takes its place when an unplanned turning is made?

I had *always* wanted to sail around the world. Having been born in the British Isles, I had inherited a historic attitude about the oceans of the world. They became my new achievement.

We were able to afford to have a seventy-one-foot ocean-racing ketch built at Southern Ocean Shipyards in Poole, Dorset, England. A splendid Scottish doctor had advised me to "buy a boat, pull some lines, catch your balance, and you should get better." That was all I needed to turn long-wished-for plans into a reality.

Some plan, eh? Especially for someone who was a little nervous of water, having nearly drowned twice. Also, I recalled the first sailing trip with my love in the ice-encrusted river

"Dovey" in North Wales. That was a horrid experience: it was cold, very uncomfortable, and the constant tipping, definitely not my idea of fun! Now Graham wanted to sail around the WORLD with our baby Kareena (she was only two years old), Andy who was nearly twelve, and Tessa, almost sixteen!

Well, it was his life dream. I was willing to try to be brave. I could swim, and so could all the children. This would be an adventure all right, and wasn't I the one who loved adventure? So we were off.

On March 2, 1971, the yacht *Treena* began her twenty-four-thousand-mile voyage under our ownership. In her day, she was one of only a few large production yachts made. She embodied all that was really first class about British yacht building. She was lovely, but she held a family that was not yet able to love. Appearance blended into achievement, and for two years that was enough; but in the end, even the momentum of self seems to lessen.

Been there, done that — so, what's next?

What was next would break us out of an endless series of storms into the fair weather of faith.

Locust Grove, 1975 — Graham and Treena, within weeks of their Christian walk

CHAPTER EIGHTEEN: LOCUST GROVE

I was so attracted to the house,
T'was a gift from above,
Which it was to be, eventually,
For there we found true love.

We had sailed twenty-four thousand miles and had only run aground once, in Montreal.

In 1973, we did it again, at the joining of Peach Blossom Creek and the Tred Avon River on the Chesapeake Bay in Maryland's eastern shore. It is said of the Chesapeake that only two kinds of people haven't run aground there — those who are liars and those who've never been there!

We drew nine feet and we were stuck hard. Across the calm, quiet creek, there was a lovely white three-story colonial house with six pillars, surrounded by huge trees, rolling lawns, and an enormous new dock. It was September and the leaves were still full and green. The house sparkled.

"What a lovely house!" Treena almost clapped her hands. I agreed in passing but was preoccupied with working out when we might edge our way off the mud bank. Over the next hour or so, Treena continued to gaze and smile. Treena had never ever been an acquisitive person. I was quite enough for one family; there really was no need! And yet, here she was *loving* that house!

Frankly, my achievement goal was to circumnavigate. I dearly wanted to sail under Sydney Harbor Bridge and look up at *that* Penthouse from my own luxurious floating platform.

"I'll tell you what," I suggested. "Since we are stuck here for at least another four hours, why don't I row ashore and make him an offer for it?" I thought it was a fun idea — not really serious.

"You wouldn't," Treena laughed. "Would you?"

"Sure, but don't be surprised if the owner chases me off with a gun after he hears the kind of offer we can afford." We laughed together, and I set off for the dock.

I knocked at the back door, and a pleasant nondescript man opened it with slightly raised eyebrows. "Yes?" I offered him my hand, which he shook firmly.

"I'm from that yacht over there. We've been admiring your house," I said.

"Oh, yes. I see. Well, I've been admiring your boat. Er, what can I do for you?"

"Do you have a gun? A large one?" I asked.

"Would a duck gun do?" he replied with a slight frown.

"Perfect! Could you chase me down the dock with it?" I asked with a slight smile.

"Why should I do that?" He was now clearly perturbed. I explained about my promise to Treena and that she would be watching.

"OK. So make your offer." He seemed to understand.

"Do I *have* to do that?" I reasoned, "After all, what I can offer isn't very much and deserves the chase." I really didn't want to seem silly.

"Offer — or no gun," he said firmly.

I offered him $240,000 for a ten-thousand-foot 1814 (original building) colonial in nine acres of lawn with more than six hundred feet of waterfront!

"You're right." He didn't smile. "That is worth the chase down the dock. But just for my fun, how soon could you provide that in cash?"

I called our accountant in New York and got an answer.

"By Tuesday." I held my hand over the phone. He reached over his desk and offered me his hand. I took it. He shook it.

"Then it's yours," he said seriously.

I have no idea why he decided to sell. All kinds of wild ideas have surfaced over the years, but none that have proved correct. I rowed back out to the *Treena*.

"I didn't see anyone chase you," Treena cried out from the boat. "Wasn't the owner in?" she asked.

"No, not exactly," I replied as I reached the boat and looked up at her. "You see, you are the new owner."

Well, you could have knocked me down with a feather, as they say in the UK. A house! Somewhere to live that didn't sway from side to side. A place that was dry, even in wet weather, on solid green ground. I whooped, sang, danced, then suddenly stopped. I realized that this was good-bye to Mickel and Tin Tin, our wonderful crew, who had become such good friends. Nevertheless, I had schools to find, curtains to make (which were, incidentally, twelve feet high and fourteen feet across). I had never made curtains before! However, I made eighty-

six! Yes, I did! And each one of them was lined!

I bought a sewing machine, a book on how to make curtains, and some very expensive material. The man who sold me all the materials suggested that I should get them made by a professional. "No!" I said. "I'll let you come and critique them when I've finished. That's the reason I bought this lovely material — so I would have to make them perfectly." He smiled!

After six weeks, I had finished them all. I asked the man to come and see them and hang them for me. He was amazed. The curtains were great, and I knew the house felt cared for. We did find good schools for all our children, and all was well for awhile.

We still had to face our troubles from the past; they were under the surface, always ready to bob to the top. One can't run away from trouble; it's always there. Little did we know what was in store for us all.

Our circumnavigation of the world had stopped, and eventually we sold *Treena* and applied to live and work in the United States — especially because we now had a house there.

I never did get to sail under Sydney Harbor Bridge in my own luxury yacht, but we had moved into the house, in which all things would become new.

"I go [ahead] to prepare a place for you."
JOHN 14:2

CHAPTER NINETEEN: THERE'S A PLACE SOMEWHERE

Do not trust anymore, it turns to dust.
Mammon was not what we needed.
We had to trust wisely, yet our time to do this,
we never heeded.

During our time at sea, we left our affairs in the hands of the vice president of a very large and respected accounting firm in New York. We had invested in a Mormon-owned development company through a fellow yachtsman whom we admired. His Mormon lifestyle (if you excluded the luxury yacht) appeared to be beyond reproach.

Unfortunately, he proved to have a dark side and was convicted of fraud and sent to a federal prison for several years. While this was happening, our financial guy in New York contracted cancer, and our file went unsupervised during the decline and fall of our investment. As a result, we, like many others in the mid-1970s who had invested in real estate, lost it *all*.

We had lost a very large part of the income that we had saved from *The Galloping Gourmet*'s worldwide success and, therefore, needed to go back to work. We also desperately needed to sell our very large boat at a very difficult time.

One amusing opportunity arose in the midst of this troubling time. We made an appointment to show the boat to a pleasant entrepreneur, who turned up in a stretch Mercedes, the first we had ever seen. He loved the boat and made us an offer that I was immediately able to refuse. He offered us shares in a private company that was to go public "shortly."

You will recall that we had really liked and respected the Mormon yachtsman and our New York advisor! I took another look at the stretch Mercedes and, feeling very much the wiser for our experiences, politely declined.

The nice man in the Mercedes did eventually take his company public, and called it Sprint! At one point, I worked it out that his shares would have amounted to fourteen million dollars for our boat. Which, of course, I had rejected. And like all (or most) big boat owners, we eventually sold at a considerable loss.

■ ■ ■ ■

Looking back over this time, both Treena and I seriously doubt that we would have gone back to television had it not been for these repetitive financial disasters. We also wonder, had all this not happened, if we would have been less open, less aware of our need for assurance that we had any kind of future security.

During our ocean voyaging, I discovered a new way of eating. People used to say, "Who owns this beautiful yacht?" To which our crew would reply, "The tall guy in the yellow slickers, hanging over the line." I had found out, the hard way, that in my case, a very high fat, gourmet lifestyle can cause seasickness of seemingly life-threatening dimension.

We changed our way of eating and literally embraced a lifestyle that greatly improved our health. We were so encouraged by the changes that, when we got ashore and we became aware of our financial need, we put the two together and came up with a new television series of just four minutes duration called *Take Kerr.* Because we pronounce our name "care," we at least felt it a clever title!

This was the start of a whole new career path for me — one in which taste, aroma, color, and texture became more important than butter, wine, elegant sauces, and large portions of well-marbled meat.

The series, which played for several years during CNN's early days, explored how to major in the creative and minor in the destructive. This was three years before the first U.S. Government Dietary Guidelines were published in 1978. We were well ahead of the curve, at least in terms of the public's level of awareness of the need.

Take Kerr went very well, and before long, after several series of sixty-five episodes each, we had begun to repair our financial situation.

This, however, did nothing to resolve Treena's ongoing personal problems. You could draw a pretty straight line back through Treena's life to get a clear picture of her enormous need. Her early years are greatly revealed in part by her poem.

POEM
Said my father to me when I was small
"Be the best, my daughter, the best of all.
The best student, swimmer, whatever you do.
Always be better than the best of the few.
At all times be first, but never scrape through.

Then mummy and I will be proud of you."
Now my mother taught me to
"Never complain,
Whatever the hurt, whatever the pain!
More often than not, it's imagination.
Hypochondria is an abomination."
These were my lessons to be a success,
But I knew I couldn't be better and best.
I'd not even try to do any new things
For I would let others down with my failings.
Failure must not be allowed or permitted.
Thus, success for me was strictly limited.

What a burden my life became. I obeyed and obliged as much as I could. I wanted to be loved, but I really had to perform for it. My childhood trials pushed self-worth further and further away, until I truly believed that I was a nothing! However, I would discover that forgiveness would heal past pain and dim the memory.

We had met before these childhood trials and married afterward, *almost* leaving behind its long-lasting impact on our lives.

In Australia, my green, composite-fiber suitcase wasn't the only lasting symbol that I discarded, and my unfaithfulness as her husband was salt rubbed into her childhood wounds.

The accident on U.S. 101 had shaken her

badly, leading to a tuberculosis and lung resection. Her postoperative recuperation introduced her to a range of pharmaceuticals that seemed to smooth out the mountainous ups and downs of her tortured life. There was Valium for anxiety, Mogadon for sleeplessness, Benzedrine for listlessness, and Darvon for the initial pain — and the ongoing need for the buzz.

Strangely, here we were again. On the outside, our career had resumed its upward vertical trend, while on the inside life simply couldn't have been worse.

My life was getting worse and worse, more and more frightening. I saw children's heads roll into the road as I drove past, bridges collapsed, sending screeching metal below. My temper was now a rage of rejection. Life was a constant turmoil and frustration. I took uppers and downers and sleeping pills; I always hoped I wouldn't wake up. I "oommed" my way through transcendental meditation and Yoga. I twisted and turned my body this way and that and would scream if somebody interrupted me. "Go away! I'm getting peace!" However, nothing, absolutely nothing worked.

After one especially troubling event, I went for a long walk along the marshy foreshore of the Tred Avon, wondering what else I could possibly do to improve our lives together in what was now a large and hate-filled house.

An idea surfaced and then resurfaced. I hated it, refused it, but it wouldn't go away. I was the cause. Treena's condition was the effect. The only recourse was to remove the cause. I had to go.

Later, during a time of relative peace, I broached my idea. It was the most desperate of moments. I was torn in two: One part resisted mightily; *I couldn't live without her.* The other part loved her enough to let her go.

I offered to help her make a new life without me. She replied, "I'll go upstairs and think about it." She left without looking back and without protest of any kind.

I sat in my study watching the darkening day in the late fall, seeing only the dead and dying of the season — and of my life.

I heard her coming back down the stairs and then felt her hand on my shoulder and the rustle of paper as she handed me a poem.

"I wrote this for you. It's my answer." Her voice was very quiet and soft. I began to read:

to be aware, and love in faith
is all one should desire.

195

to try; to learn; and rectify,
some seeming wrong, this should be done.
yet do not be alone, for when two love
one is half if left, or leaves the arms
of one whose life is stressed.
i prefer to be complete and
walk with you along the street
toward the other half of self.
to learn with you, to help, to understand
the way we lost ourselves.
we have the right to right the wrongs
to each we've made. no one alone is wrong,
no one alone is right; in marriage, we are one
and love is ours — not flight.

I went to see Treena's doctor once again. "Is there any medication that could help?" I pleaded. We'd tried Yoga, transcendental meditation, and all kinds of applications from our esoteric Buddhist background (somewhat inherited from my parents' odd collection of religions), and nothing had even "touched" the growing urgency of her needs.

"Probably," he replied. "There is nothing more that I can do. What she needs is a time apart. She needs to be voluntarily committed to a mental institution for an indeterminate period."

I will *never* forget these words. I *knew* I was

a major cause. I had offered her relief. Now here was her doctor confirming the separation, *for a reason.* This gave me a flicker of hope.

"When?" I asked.

"Let's revisit this after Christmas," he offered.

We had less than two months. Treena had no idea of the deadline; only I was the one who counted the days and could see no other recourse.

It was then that Ruthie arrived.

Locust Grove, 1975 — Treena and Graham, eyes closed intentionally, on the dock as they began their walk of faith

CHAPTER TWENTY:
THE WITNESS IN WHITE

My little black angel dressed in white
Kept us all within her sight, unto this very day.

There was a knock on our front door. I answered it. Ruthie.

She was black, dressed entirely in white. Her eyes shone. She smiled shyly.

"Do you need a maid?" she blurted, and before I could answer, she went on hurriedly.

"I'm not a maid. I'm a missionary, but our church is too small to send me. I want to help my brothers and sisters in Haiti. My pastor, he says, go find some rich folks who live down by the water and get a good wage and put it aside in the bank until you've got enough to go." She stopped suddenly and looked up with those shining eyes for an answer.

"Can you speak their French patois?" I asked with a slight challenge.

"No, sir," she replied readily. "But I've got a strong back and willin' hands, and I got Jesus in my heart."

I felt exactly like a galleon under full sail that had suddenly lost all the wind. My parents had had a pub next door to a church in England. But nobody who dropped in for a drink after church *ever* said they "had Jesus in their heart!"

I called to Treena. Did she have a need for a maid?

We looked at each other and then at Ruthie, still so small, so black and white. We knew *our* needs; perhaps *somehow* she might help.

We had never had a housemaid before. I had always done my own work. I looked at her and something inside me knew she would be right. I had always loved black people in any country, and then there was the way she smiled at me.

RUTHIE
She smiled at me
I knew she knew.
Innocently she did stand,
Stretching out
Her small black hand.
She arrived and "gleamed"
With the knowledge glowing

From large brown eyes.
Without music, she seemed to sing.
Angels must have sang her praises,
For her precious "faith bouquet"
Were the silent prayers
She prayed for me.

We invited her in.

Ruthie couldn't speak French, and she was certainly unfamiliar with the violent language being used in our house. So she did what she did best. She prayed.

Ruthie lived with us during the week and traveled back to Wilmington, Delaware, on weekends to attend her church, the Holy Church of Mount Zion. It was a Pentecostal Holiness church of about seventy souls, all African American from the inner city. All of them believed strongly in Jesus and prayer. At Ruthie's request, they began to pray for the white lady with troubles who lived in the big white house by the water.

After the first month they moved to the creation of a prayer chain, with a sign-up sheet to cover each hour of a twenty-four-hour day, seven days a week — our first brush with 24/7.

Then they prayed *and* fasted.

Ruthie simply served us quietly and well.

"Make it your ambition to lead a quiet life, to mind your own business and to work with your hands, . . . so that your daily life may win the respect of outsiders. . . ."
1 THESSALONIANS 4:11–12 NIV

She earned our respect.

Can there be any greater miracle? Can science or any human endeavor compete with the transformation of the heart that begins the process we call *sanctification?* We all know that man can do truly extraordinary, mind-boggling feats. The cause and effects of those actions are staggering in their application.

But what of the spirit of man? For all our technical breakthroughs, are we more loving, more joyful, more at peace, kinder, gentler, more faithful, and, dare I add, more self-controlled? Remember the Oliver Wendell Holmes quote? "I wouldn't give you a fig for simplicity this side of complexity, but I would give my life for simplicity on the other side of complexity."

Has our modern, advanced, developed, technically managed lifestyle become *too* complex? If so, how do we reach for simplicity?

Oliver Wendell Holmes declared his unwillingness to give a fig for *anything* that promised to bring simplicity to complexity. Somehow, he *knew,* as many of us probably already know, that there is another lifestyle search that begins by putting the complexity of our modern age behind us, and that this carries an oddly triumphant decision along with its adoption. We will, to some extent, lose our lives in order to gain our heart's desire for — simplicity?

This is the only decision that can, for a season or so, hold back the mudslide of modernity. No matter how much whitewash is poured into its stream, it is still a vain attempt to bypass the great commandment, in order to redirect our love and appreciation toward our own effort, for our own purposes.

"There is a way that seems right to a man,
but in the end it leads to death."

PROVERBS 16:25 NIV

CHAPTER TWENTY-ONE: GUANO — LEST YOU FORGET!

*Guano, a fertilizer, a special fertilizer
to enrich the mind
Of Gra that God was calling to Himself,
so he would see.*

We have already discussed our agreement to become witnesses for Jesus Christ in the courts of public opinion. Should you need to refresh your memory, you may find our accounts in chapter 11.

You may notice that not only are we clearly different as man and woman, but our individual needs were enormous, pressing, and baffling. We were reasonably intelligent, successful, and yet desperate for a solution. We could afford to buy the best of man-made counsel, but none of it even came close to meeting our needs. Perhaps one reason was, in my case, I had no real idea what my needs were, other than my reconciliation with Treena.

The other reason might never have occurred to us — that we needed to be *of one mind* about our faith. How could we be of one mind when we didn't know what we believed? Our faith was a work-in-progress. We were searching, blazing a trail in a feel-good forest along pathways beaten flat by blind guides.

Now, here we were, the forest behind us and one narrow pathway leading directly into a bright horizon. Treena had written about this moment in her prophetic poem.

I prefer to be complete
and walk with you along the street
toward the other half of self.

We shared the same pathway. We could come to more fully understand its destination, but, for the moment, it remained littered with the debris of the past. All things would *become* new, but it would take time.

Many years later, we would read Paul's letter to the Corinthians that made complete sense to us. "A woman who has an unbelieving husband, and he consents to live with her, she must not send her husband away. For the unbelieving husband is sanctified through his wife, . . . for otherwise your children are unclean, but now they are holy" (1

Cor. 7:13–14).

We firmly believe that we were called to walk this narrow pathway of faith *together;* and when we see or stumble over our past mistakes, we should stop and take the time to throw them to one side, lest others also stumble. "Go through, go through the gates; clear the way for the people; build up, build up the highway; remove the stones, lift up a standard over the peoples" (Isa. 62:10).

Looking back now to those heady first days when everything seemed so bright and new and possible and secure, I would have loved to have known that God's will for us both (and for every believer new or mature) is that we be individually *sanctified.*

"Understand what the will of the LORD is."
EPHESIANS 5:17
"This is the will of God, your sanctification."
1 THESSALONIANS 4:3

At this point in my writing, I put this manuscript aside and picked up my reference books to do a word study on *sanctification.* I felt I knew *roughly* what it meant but needed to know for sure.

This is what I found, first from *Webster's Dictionary:*

a. to make holy; specifically
    (a) to set apart as holy; consecrate
    (b) to make free from sin; purify
b. to make binding or inviolable by a religious sanction
c. to make productive of spiritual blessing.

In Young's *Analytical Concordance of the Bible,* I found both the Hebrew and Greek words to hold the same meaning: *gadesh* and *hagiasmos,* "to be separate or set apart."

We were, it seems, being set apart for God's purposes.

The first piece of rubble I fell over was literally my *stuff* and how I thought it made me look to others.

Our arrival, as resident aliens to the United States back in 1974, was accompanied by a whole welter of complications both legal and financial. Buried in the midst of these was an almost silly technicality to do with dates.

I found the relevant papers late on Friday afternoon and immediately called our *new* accountant. He was away for a long weekend. I called our lawyer. He was tied up on a case.

It *seemed* that everything we had done to repair our finances was at risk *if* we hadn't taken a specific step by a specific date! The easy part about it was that nobody would know unless they asked, and that was extremely unlikely. Then Treena asked the hard question.

"If they did ask, what would you say?"

I could easily *fudge* the dates to fall to our favor. Nobody would know and nobody would be hurt.

"But, if you *fudged* them," she said firmly, "or lied," she added, "then how do you think God would feel?"

I went off for a walk around the garden to resolve this issue. What I needed was a clever compromise. As I walked, it felt as though the clouds gathered and darkened immediately above my head. I couldn't duck the issue. It was either the truth or a lie!

"But you can't want that, God," I cried out. "Not after all the effort to rebuild our financial security!"

No reply!

So, I took my Bible and sat under a bushy evergreen down by the water's edge and faced into the setting sun that reflected off the river like a pathway of gold. I *half* expected to see Jesus walking up that path to give me my way of escape.

He didn't.

I had heard that some people actually close their eyes, flicking the Bible pages, come to a stop, and jab the page with a finger (prayerfully, of course). I tried it and got the *index.*

Then I got my answer. A bird, resting above my head, chose that precise God-ordained moment to relieve itself onto my forehead and my Bible, lest I would ever forget! And lest you feel that I presume upon God as the author of this "anointing," may I add that my replacement Bible that I use every day (dated January 1991, sixteen years after the event) has a similar bird dropping ingrained on the leather cover — *lest I forget?*

I went indoors with my evidence, and through our laughter, I let Treena know that the only answer I could give would have to be the truth, regardless of the consequences. The sun came out; the clouds were smaller, white, and fluffy!

On Monday both our lawyer and our consultant returned my desperate Friday calls. "Mr. Kerr, we thought that we had written to you on the matter. We discussed it with the authorities. Since it was only a minor technicality, we were told it didn't apply in your case."

I had stumbled over my "stuff" only to find that it had never been at risk. What *had* been at risk was my witness. Would I choose to tell the truth, the whole truth, and nothing but the truth *so help me, God?*

■ ■ ■ ■

This dramatic encounter led swiftly to our first opportunity to move beyond *guano* in our ability to "hear" God. We doubt that there is anything more potentially divisive than the declaration that "we have heard from God and He said. . . ."

The best we know how to handle this experience is to phrase it in less absolute terms: "We *believe* we have heard from God. This is what we *think* He said. *What do you think?*"

Our first test came shortly after I became a witness in the spring of '75. We were going to bed after a long day, and I expressed my newly minted opinion about religious issues to my patient wife: "I don't think God actually speaks on a personal basis." I explained, "It's really a matter of something we've read in the Bible that comes to our minds and it . . . well, it *feels* like He has spoken!" I said this on my way to the bathroom to get Treena a glass of water.

As I filled the glass, an *idea* came into my head. I returned to the bedroom and stopped for a moment at the foot of the bed. "What do you think of this?" I asked Treena. "The true face of Satan is the compromiser."

Treena thought about it for a moment or two and then asked, "So, where in the Bible did you read that?"

The hair actually stirred on the back of my neck — well, it seemed like it!

"You mean that that might have been God?" I asked incredulously.

"Tell you what," Treena suggested. "Why don't we ask our new pastor?"

Our pastor took it all very seriously.

"It isn't a specific verse. But it's certainly a truth-filled statement if the compromise means speaking or living out a falsehood."

We went away with our first personal word and made up a seal like that used by a notary public that stamps papers with an embossed authority. It read "Jesus Without Compromise." We had begun our journey with a public declaration, a banner fully visible to those who chose to observe our passing.

We now feel quite certain that when we make public declarations or protestations about our relationship with God that this *must be tested.*

Surely God doesn't want a false witness. It is abundantly clear that He hates hypocrisy and will have the truth shouted from the rooftops rather than have His standards compromised. We were about to be tested.

CHAPTER TWENTY-TWO:
I WANT A CREDIT
IN YOUR TV SHOWS

Our slogan, "Jesus Without Compromise,"
would of course be tested.
T'would try our faith, shock the media,
and make some rather heated.
This was not the way of stars; compromise
they must, or go!
Go we did. We'd won this time, but later
t'was not so!

During this extraordinary period of change, I had an overlapping experience that would lead to what seemed at the time to be the ultimate test of our declaration to live for "Jesus Without Compromise." I was invited by the dean of the world-famous Hotel School at Cornell University in Ithaca, New York, to become an adjunct professor. I was enormously flattered. What an honor and an opportunity to give back to an industry that had so graciously given so much to me over my entire life.

It was during my "tenure" that I became a witness. In the fall of '75, I was up early and shaving. With nothing better to do, I decided to shave off half the foam *exactly*. I left the right side smothered in white, the left side scraped clean — not a trace of lather.

When I'd finished smiling at the result, I got that feeling I was being spoken to. "I want a credit on your television show."

Now, I laughed outright, pointed my finger at my half-shaved face, and declared, "That's you, buddy, not God! The God who created the universe and all things in it doesn't need to have a credit on a cooking show!"

The simple request echoed on and on through the rest of the day and continued like a celestial commercial jingle that I couldn't get out of my head.

Less than a week later, I was in Ithaca at the university teaching on "moral ethics in the hotel and restaurant industry." My class was the second largest on campus; only the deans had more students. When the bell rang to end my session, I invited my students to come back after hours to an announcement I wanted to make.

"I know your parents sent you to Cornell to gain a first-class education. If you come back this evening, I have something to say that isn't directly what they (or you) paid for."

Perhaps it was the mystery or my *then* celebrity, but more than four hundred of my six hundred class returned. I shared what little I knew about my Christian conversion. I was greeted with a more or less stunned silence and no questions.

The very next morning, the dean sent for me.

"I've had a complaint from two of the students who came to your ad hoc lecture last night," he said gravely. "Perhaps you are not aware that this is a state-funded institution and, as such, unlike several other universities, we do not permit religious teaching on campus." He seemed confident that I would understand, but I apparently didn't get it.

"I didn't *teach*, Dean. I simply shared a very personal experience that changed my life and can do nothing else but change my way of teaching." It was now my turn to feel confident that he would understand — he didn't.

"I share your faith. I'm also a Christian," he explained. "But, like many others who teach here, I've had to accept that I need to *compromise*." He went on at some length, but I was left stranded on that one word.

Compromise!

The true face of Satan is the compromiser, and we had adopted the slogan *Jesus Without Compromise!* Would this simply be a slogan, or was it a deeply engaged commitment?

"So, what's your decision?" the dean demanded. I came back to the room with a bump. "Come on," he urged. "Will you continue to teach, or leave?"

"Well, Dean," I said. I felt both certain and uncertain. Much like a salmon facing a waterfall, I had to keep going or settle where I was.

I leapt.

"Then I must leave, Dean. I'm sorry if this causes you any embarrassment," I added lamely.

He wasn't pleased. Somehow my decision must have sounded like an accusation leveled at his career choice. It's the only reason I can give for his displeasure.

"I'm upset by this because you are a genius, and you're throwing your life away on a religious whim." I had never even remotely come close to being called a *genius* before (or since!). So, it had the opposite effect than the one intended.

My decision to follow Jesus hadn't required a giant intellect. All it had taken was one deeply frustrated question: "What do I have to say to get to know You like Treena does?"

The dean didn't leave it there. He called out after us. I was with Treena at the time. "I'm S-A-V-E-D. I am S-A-V-E-D. I'm . . ." He did this in a singsong alphabet down a main corridor among students at a break. Neither of us could work out what he was saying, so we turned back.

"What is it, Dean? What are you spelling?" Treena asked.

"I'm SAVED. I'm SAVED," he yelled at her, his face quite flushed.

"Oh, I'm so glad to hear that," Treena replied with her sweetest, most innocent smile.

That was not nearly the end of it. We received an official letter demanding that we "remove all references to [our] connection with the university." Our publishers and our television production company were also advised.

We had acknowledgments in our books and a credit on the TV show *Take Kerr — a credit on the television show*. There was that *jingle* again, but that had been more than two weeks ago!

Our old credit had read, "We are grateful for assistance provided by Cornell University." How would we change that to, "We are grateful for assistance provided by God"?

There was no way that wasn't a witness; it

was more like an enema!

We asked a Christian friend, Ron Hembre, who, as a pastor, worked on script development for a faith-based television network. "How do we give God a credit?"

"You could use His Word. A simple Bible reference would do," he suggested. "You could keep on changing it. God's good at broadcasting seed."

We did just that. On each episode, where once we had a two-second credit for Cornell, we now had a one-second reference that appeared at the bottom of the screen in quite small type: 1 THESS. 4:11.

One second, and all hell broke loose!

We received notification through J. Walter Thompson, the world's largest advertising agency, which distributed our programs, that "a large station in Chicago" had complained about the Scripture credit. We were instructed to remove it forthwith.

"I want a credit on your TV shows."
"Jesus Without Compromise."

Add up the words. There's only eleven, and there was nothing ambiguous about any of them.

We replied in what we still believe was (to us) a genuinely nonargumentative manner.

"We feel we are supposed to have the Scripture credit there and can't really compromise what we've done."

We heard nothing until another three months when we were back in studio with another sixty-five episodes ready to record.

The cameras were ready to roll when a gray-flannel-suited advertising executive came on the set with an official demand. "You are not to include the Scripture reference on this series." He used all the authority of his undoubted power as the sponsors' representative.

"I'm sorry," I explained, "but we have already corresponded on this, and we can't compromise the credit." I offered a weak smile.

"But you've done all this work for the new series. You can't just close down and walk!" He was not in a smiling mood.

"If you want to call a halt, that's OK with us." I was in the midst of a great calm, listening in to my own voice.

"God knows exactly how we can use the research. There's plenty of need for it in other media." I still had the smile. Perhaps it was the smile that caused him to explode.

"All right, then. If you *must* have your little God thing." He turned abruptly and stormed out of the studio, his gray flannels flapping.

We made that series and returned home to prepare for the next.

"Daddy, did you do the tomato paste episode in the last series?" Our daughter, Tess, was watching television.

"Yes, darling," I called back. "Why?"

"'Cause it didn't have a Scripture credit."

I called New York to let our coproducers hear the news.

"Yes, we know," Paul replied. "We agreed with J. Walter Thompson to have the Scripture credit edited out." He paused. "We thought that by now you would have come to your senses and understood the practical issues involved."

We requested that the credit be replaced and assured him that our spiritual senses appeared to have remained intact. We were amazed when we were told that the credits would be replaced. But there was a condition.

"In future series, you will agree to make no references whatsoever to your personal faith."

This was more than the credit; it was a blanket agreement. We politely, but firmly, turned it down and began to wonder what

God had in store for us. We were just forty-one years old and had to continue to pay the bills.

"Graham." It was Paul back on the phone. "If you do this, I will be in a very serious financial situation. All those who helped you become famous would be seriously hurt. We are all so pleased for you and Treena. Your decision has obviously been of great benefit to your lives. But why should your new faith have to cause us so much harm?"

He was right, of course. Why should it? We had a contract. We had changed and wanted everything to be as new as we were (or felt).

We prayed earnestly. "What do we do now?" We believe the Lord answered with a question: "What do they want of you?"

"They want money; they need ongoing cash flow," I replied.

"What do you want from Me?" Again, the lightest of volume.

"To know You better," I replied.

"Then give them the money and follow Me."

I looked at Treena and she looked back. Our eyes didn't meet — they merged.

"What do you think about giving Paul all our rights and royalties to all we've ever done with them, and the name *Galloping*

Gourmet?" As I put it into words, my mind raced back over all the work we'd done, and then it raced forward over what life might be like without income!

I began to cry. In a way, it hurt badly. I was scared.

And then Treena spoke. "I think that's God." She was so much at peace in the midst of watching me cry.

I had quietly prayed and just knew in my heart this was right. I was also excited that at last Psalm 81:6 (which I had believed God had given me) was now coming true. I just knew it was Him, absolutely. I didn't think about the security rug being pulled out from under us. Why would I? Jesus was our security. I believed absolutely what I had read in the Bible. (Read Hebrews 6:19. It's truly wonderful.)

Just seeing her receive what I believed I'd heard was what I needed. It was then I remembered what I had answered to the question "What do you want of Me?"

I had replied, "To know You better." To which He had replied, "Then give them the money and follow Me."

It had begun with my face half-shaved and a request for a credit on our television show, and now here we were, more than a year later, stepping out of our old obligated life with its solid financial base into absolutely uncharted waters.

I picked up the phone to call Paul. When I had finished explaining that we would not be able to comply with the agency's demand to be "silent Christians," he began to almost plead. "You don't understand what this means to me —"

I interrupted. "Oh, yes, Paul, we believe we do. And this, we feel, is the solution." I recounted what we believed God had said to us.

There was silence.

"Is this what people mean by Christianity?" he asked.

"Well, we've only been Christians for a short while. But I guess it means that if you hear God tell you to do something, then you do it."

At this moment in recording our journey, we began to wrestle with *numbers.* Exactly how much did we relinquish by the decision to give up our rights?

At first, the problem was the word *exactly* because that would be the most difficult issue to answer. There were known funds that were due to us — ongoing contracts that had value for their term and possible renewals. There were book and program royalties, and then there was the value of the brand name *Galloping Gourmet.* Of course, some of those depended upon what others would be able to do with those assets to turn them, for example, into another Betty Crocker or Emeril.

Looking back over those years, it appears that less was achieved than had been hoped, and, therefore, how *exactly* does one measure the relinquishment? We have chosen to explain our predicament and now, in the interest of known truth, to avoid it. We just don't know. What we do know is that we listed everything we knew that we'd achieved with them and gave it all.

The act of faith in letting go of our future security wasn't as difficult to do in that full tide of belief that we were hearing God's voice.

The tide stayed up until the relentless demands of cash flow began to make the tide go out.

You may recall that we had worked hard to rebuild our financial foundations and had begun to do so with the very programs and books that we had just given away. We were, however, left with the costs of maintaining the huge house, boats, cars — the list goes on and on. What reserves we had would soon be exhausted unless we moved!

We had believed God to say, "Give them the money and follow Me." So we were ready to follow, but where and how? Finances were pressing. We had to decide, or did we?

In the very first chapter of the book of Acts, Jesus tells His disciples to *wait* in Jerusalem until the Holy Spirit fills them, and then to go out with the kingdom message. "Wait," "receive," "go" was the supernatural sequence, and remains so until the days in which we now live.

I didn't wait, and I now know that I didn't receive; but we did go, and we had to live with the consequences for several tough years.

CHAPTER TWENTY-THREE:
THROUGH PRESUMPTION
COMES NOTHING
BUT STRIFE

The effrontery, the audacity,
the impertinence, the nerve.
Logic nullified faith, yet no crossbow fired,
no arrow curved.

I enjoy the human exercise of logic. To me it's treating a problem like a jigsaw puzzle. There's always a sequence. Turn all the pieces color side up, find all the straight edges, locate the right-angled corners, and collect the pieces into light, shade, and primary colors. Then you can begin to fit the pieces as you check out the finished picture on the box.

That's logical, but simply flip through the Bible and you'll see that God almost *never* works that way!

We don't have a completed picture of our lives to check out, and most pieces remain color side *down*. If it were not so, we'd have no need of faith, which is the belief in things *not* seen. *Logic can be a bad leader.* It was in our case!

I am rather opposed to logic most of the time. My belief is that if God said it, it is so. I think most women are this way. Most men I know are logical. I remember praying in a group that consisted mostly of men. The wife of the leader and myself went to the Lord immediately without any facts or discussion. But the men had to make sure they had all the facts first before they prayed with us. THEN we prayed! We all heard and we were in agreement. So, logic for some men obviously can work, yet certainly not always. Logic can be dangerous and may even displace faith at times, as you will see.

If we were to follow God, then it should surely be to serve people!

Then how should we serve?

There was always my ability to cook and Treena's ability to produce, but we had burned our media bridges behind us.

After a whole year and a half, I still had confidence in the Word. Psalm 81:6 says, "I removed his shoulder from the burden: his hands were delivered from the pots" (KJV).

We agreed together that once we had set

our hands on the plough we shouldn't look back. The truth was that we didn't want to go back. We wanted a whole new spiritual life, and we wanted it NOW, before we were engulfed by our expenses.

So, if it wasn't food or media, what was it?

We had been comforted as a couple. Our marriage and our love for one another had been restored *overnight*. So why not look for others whose lives were wrecked and who faced divorce? Would they give God a chance to repair their lives as He had ours?

All we would need to do was to provide a place in which this could happen and to be there for them if needed.

Simple, logical, and biblical.

We began to look for a place apart. It seemed to us that a remote area would provide a sense of adventure (*now there's a straight edge*). How about the Rocky Mountains, with the awesome grandeur so often associated with the divine. *Another straight edge.*

We traveled to Colorado in the spring of 1975 and found a verdant valley under Castle Peak watered by Milk Creek. There was one established house and a rough road in thirty thousand acres of nothing!

We "put out a fleece" that held a long list

of logical straight edges, including price, zoning regulations, water rights. We then pushed past logic and prayed to see if God wanted to add to our list.

He did!

"Take a bow and arrow and stand beside the house facing Castle Peak. Draw back the bow with all your strength, aim high, and release the arrow. Where the arrow lands, dig down to find a wellspring that will not fail. This shall be as a sign."

Our long list of logical fleece issues were all fully met, and in the press of time, we couldn't locate a bow and arrow (and at the time it seemed a little silly!). We did, however, clear an upper-level creek that would flow over the very ground that the arrow might have reached — so?

So, we did it! We purchased the valley and laid out our plans for a village called "Rejoice."

Chapter Twenty-Four: The Garage Sale

"Sell all you have and follow me,"
said Jesus to the rich young leader.
Thus we did: We sold our property, stuff, and
every acre.

I'm wondering if you recall the nature of my very own miracle — the one where, unknown to me at the time, God had flipped the switch and turned off the lights that were my constant source of reward for all my labors. My stuff had ceased to satisfy my needs for reward. I found that I was serving my stuff, and I got nothing in return. It was with this understanding that we planned to have a massive "garage sale" that some folks would upgrade to read "estate sale."

Because we needed the money to begin our development of the village, we thought it prudent to pray. Once again, we were surprised by what we felt that we heard. "You are to obtain the services of an auctioneer who will agree to conduct the auction and will donate his fee."

This would prove to be the most humbling act of our new lives. No, really, it was the most humbling of my entire life to date!

I located the phone numbers of seven auction houses in Maryland and began to call them. "Why, yes, Mr. Kerr, we would be delighted to be of service. Our firm has done estate sales for more than one hundred years for the finest families. You need to have us donate our fees? Why, of course, we can allow a small percentage . . . *all* of our fees? Really, Mr. Kerr" . . . *click!*

And that's the way it went, until auctioneer number seven, who did mostly agricultural equipment sales for perfectly ordinary people. He promised to come and see. He came and he saw.

"You've got an impressive sale here," he said as he completed the tour of our home and its stuff. "I like the awards, the gold medals, the cups — they'll do well." His mind was working overtime; you could almost hear it clink.

"Well," I hesitated, because he was our last resort, "we feel that God doesn't want to use the money obtained through the sale of idols, and those awards were idols to me at the time." I paused to see if the word *God* would make him flinch.

It didn't. I decided to risk it.

"We also believe that . . . er . . . God" — I was now getting used to a seemingly inevitable rejection — "that God . . . asked that the auctioneer donate his services." I waited in what now seemed total silence for his reply.

"You mean God spoke to you?" he asked.

"Yes," I replied defensively.

"Well, He hasn't spoken to me!" And with that he jammed his cloth cap on his head and strode out to his pickup.

I went upstairs to tell Treena that we'd lost our last auctioneer. Looking out on the drive from the upper window, I saw our last chance stop, take off his cap, scratch his head vigorously, replace the cap, and turn back toward the house. I ran down the stairs to greet him.

"He just spoke!"

That's all he said. From that moment on we had an extraordinary ally who served us brilliantly and donated his services.

We had wanted our sale to be anonymous in order to avoid somehow profiting unduly from our past celebrity. We placed an advertisement in the *very* local country paper. It was discrete to say the least. We invited people to pick up maps at a well-known intersection rather than divulge the address.

Unfortunately, this caught the attention of a news-starved editor who found out who had paid for the advertisement.

That did it! The paper used almost wartime-bold headlines on page 1: "Galloping Gourmet's Personal Effects for Sale," or words to that effect. We were inundated. The traffic backed up for four miles. A news helicopter hovered overhead and took the aerial picture you see here.

We sold *everything* — clothes, furs, jewelry, books, tapes (before CDs), furniture, cookware, china, glass . . . even old sneakers and shower curtains. There were moments,

Locust Grove — the Garage Sale

surprising ones really, when an especially valued item would sell and cause a sense of loss, but these were fleeting.

It was really funny the things that I had a tough time releasing — my music tapes, my collection of leather-bound classics (which were, to be truthful, mainly for show), and my curtains of which I was inordinately proud. Jewelry, furs, antiques, and my car brought never a twinge. We were following Jesus. The things that really hurt to see go were the gifts I had given to Graham. He was so thrilled to be obeying the Lord that he never thought of them as gifts of love. Did I bring this to his attention? Of course, but sometime later. He asked me to forgive him, which naturally I did, and the hurt was gone. There were two pictures I'd given him for his birthdays that didn't sell! God always has His own wonderful way. Isn't the Lord wonderful?

All the larger "stuff" sold: our Volvo and the ski boat, the matching Laser sailboats. We were left with two Jeep pickup trucks and several suitcases of personal working clothes and two paintings.

Later, when everyone had gone and the money was deposited, we walked through the now empty rooms, rooms that seemed to echo with our very new lives as Christians and the massive prayer and celebration meetings that used to gather on Tuesday nights. There had been a lot of good stuff among all that other stuff.

A truck came down the long drive. It was Sam, a local man who faithfully collected our trash and garden clippings once a week. "How'd your sale go?" he cried out on his way round to gather up the sacks of discarded, valueless items.

"Good, thanks, Sam — enough to help us on our way." We gave each other a hug. We felt light and somehow free and very excited about our unknown future. Sam threw the last of the black plastic sacks into his flatbed truck. As he did, we both heard the sharp clatter of metal on metal. That *might* have been the gold medal from Frankfurt Culinary Olympics and the silver cup from the MIP Television Festival at Cannes.

Both had gone out with the trash.

CHAPTER TWENTY-FIVE:
FROZEN ASSETS

God had His way finally,
by placing our nose lunettes
(A metal ring on a vehicle to which
a rope is attached for towing)
Thwarting us at every turn,
He had to freeze our last assets.
We left to join a Christian group;
we knew not what we were doing!

Without really knowing it, we had made our first series of outdulgent decisions. We had let go of our financial security in order to provide social justice to our television production team. We had now sold all our private effects in order to build a facility to serve others, and we were now giving our time to help in the same cause.

Once again, it would be such fun to share the next couple of years with you as we pounded six-inch nails through logs to complete our village, but it really doesn't explain how the seed idea of outdulgence went on to germinate, which is why this book is written.

We spent every last penny we had, and when one of our children decided to move on, we purchased their log home. All our reserves were exhausted.

We had almost completed the village and needed only a few thousand dollars for carpets and odds and ends. We wrote to the fifty or so churches we had visited in our merry-go-round testimony time to ask for help.

We received three replies. One wrote saying that they were pleased to see that God was finally dealing with us! Another wanted us to know of their change of address, and the last, for which we were grateful, offered to pray for us.

But, no money!

We were introduced to a professional fundraiser who seemed extremely confident and *really* wanted to help — that is, until we told him how much we needed. "But Mr. Kerr, a project like yours is so necessary, with almost 50 percent of Christian marriages ending in divorce. I'm sure we could raise at least two million dollars, especially using your name."

At most, we needed a little less than ten

thousand. Because his fees were 20 percent of the total raised, the prospect of earning two thousand dollars to help repair Christian marriages had reduced his level of enthusiasm considerably. He never came back!

And then it got cold, *very* cold, and it didn't snow. The ground froze, the water supply, buried seven feet down, froze, and we had to truck in water that we couldn't afford. The stream we had restored over the upper ground where the spring might have been also froze.

That's all we had — frozen assets.

I went out into the darkened valley, the night sky filled with stars, and cried out, "Why, God? What's up, God? What's up?" My voice bounded back from the cliffs and echoed round the valley.

What's up, God? What's up, God? What's up, God?

The answer came back with such clarity that it didn't need to be audible.

"You never asked Me!"

It was true — we hadn't. We were so filled with the need to move on, so sure of the logic, so certain of the confirming fleece (albeit without the arrow and the spring), that we had gone ahead without praying. We had spent our last penny, labored hard for months, had asked for help, and it had all been on our own understanding. "There is a way that seems right to a man, but in the end it leads to death" (Prov. 16:25 NIV).

We had done so much, we had all worked so hard, but every way we turned, there was trouble. Carpets for the houses were stolen, the earth froze, the water was frozen in the wells. Tessa and Joe and their baby, Matthew, left, and with them our last dollar. Naturally, they never realized this, for we never discussed it. What a shame that this wasn't where we were supposed to be. There were no doves, and we never shot the arrow. I had gone along with Graham's decisions, rather like Ananias and Sapphira, so I had to share the blame. Was it a waste of time? No, because "All things work together for the good for those who love God; and are called according to His purpose." God would use it all — every last second of what seemed to be such a complete failure!

We asked for forgiveness for our presumption and then *prayed* for our next move.

"Go down to the plains where the people are hurting."

Within days we were offered a room in a Christian home in Palms Springs, California. We packed our few things and put our frozen village up for sale. It later became an elk hunting lodge and finally a series of rustic residences for folks working in nearby Vail.

Our first attempt at an outdulgence, a giving up of self for the benefit of others, had been a complete and absolute failure because I had relied upon logic to lead us in our *spiritual* journey.

We were now back to square one with a desperate need to learn how to listen to the God to whom we had said, "We want to know You better."

Chapter Twenty-Six: Learning to Listen

Practice listening to one another,
with no interruptions, to have your say.
Then perhaps you will be ready to listen,
and hear what God has to say.

Ever since the tower of Babel, a few men have been trying to influence the course of human events by declaring that they were the ones "set apart" (at the top of the tower) to hear what God had to say with the greatest clarity.

Nothing much has changed. We are still at it — especially when we had tried to be obedient and had failed. This experience motivated us to submit to someone else to hear on our behalf!

For a season, we did just that. We wanted to know God better, so we submitted to others who had more experience, and we gave them authority over our lives. While there are good biblical bases for this kind of discipleship, it is also true that enormous harm can be done.

Because we were virtually penniless during this, our desert time, we had no recourse but to remain submitted to those in authority. There is a certain comfort to the removal of risk (or shall we say the exercise of faith?). Fortunately, in our case, God moved us on, largely because (we believe now) of our determination to "know You better." Three events came rapidly, all confirming our need to move on.

The letter from our former agent came first. One of the books we had written that had not sold well — and had been overlooked in our relinquishment of rights — had been purchased by a large publisher who wanted to reissue it at a much better price. They offered a quarter of a million dollars in advanced royalties!

We then received a check from the sale of our large home on the Chesapeake Bay. It had taken two years to find a buyer at the same price we had paid for it!

This enabled us to clear the loan for the Village of Rejoice in the mountains. The balance we gave to a couple who carried on the Rejoice Fellowship as a Christian counseling ministry in Florida. Thus, there would be ongoing "fruit."

Then, our son Andy took off to Hawaii to attend a Youth With A Mission (YWAM) Discipleship Training School (DTS).

We were enormously impressed with the changes we saw in him and wondered if we were too old for a youth ministry. As it happened, YWAM had been praying about establishing what would become their "Crossroads DTS" for folks who were forty years old and above.

All of this happened *all at once.* We were freed from financial obligations, we had a relatively small sum — rather like a bar of soap — to lather carefully, and here was an opportunity to learn how to listen, not to an interpreter or some kind of interface but *direct.*

CHAPTER TWENTY-SEVEN:
YOUTH WITH A MISSION

Were we too old to sit at the feet
and learn from those teaching His Word?
Not on your life! We were ready and willing
to learn as a child from the Lord.

Youth With A Mission (YWAM) was founded back in 1960 by Loren and Darlene Cunningham. Loren had *seen* the world covered with rippling waves of young people spreading out everywhere with the gospel message. The absolute basis of the method of communication could not have been more simple or better suited to our felt needs: "To know God and to make Him known."

We arrived and became a part of the first of their Crossroad Discipleship Training Schools at the Kailua Kona Campus of what was to become the University of the Nations.

During the years recorded in the Old Testament of the Bible, there were schools for the prophets — a nice alternative to being stoned to death for making first-time mistakes. YWAM was somewhat like these early schools but not necessarily focused on prophecy. What YWAM wanted and what we wanted was to learn to hear God and faithfully do what we believed we had been told. The remarkable aspect of their training was (and remains so) their willingness to risk failure and to readily forgive and restore those who did fail.

Time upon time, we were able to see young leaders given the opportunity to exercise their faith and to transparently celebrate and suffer the direct consequences. It was both instructive and inspiring. Treena and I spent nine years of our lives in YWAM — years in which we, along with *everyone* else, were on an individual journey of understanding.

Oh, what a lot I learned. I learned how to listen. I learned about prayer. I learned that I, Treena, was just as important to Jesus as Graham. I had things to share that were important from God. One of the biggest lessons I learned was that, if I was asked to share a truth that I believed came from the Lord, I was never to apologize. Never!

I was also taught that men and women were equal in intelligence and ability to serve the

Lord. But, perhaps best of all was Darlene Cunningham's father, Pastor Scratch. He was my mentor when I started to teach. He was such an encourager and I loved him as a father. He taught me so much about love and encouragement and speaking. I loved YWAM and always will. I was given self-worth, which was so lacking in my life, though few people, other than Graham, realized it.

Frankly, there was little time given to logic. There were few straight edges in the jigsaw puzzle of this spiritual life. It was during our initial six months of formal training that I had a life-changing experience.

Our teachers came for short sessions and often from different backgrounds and traditions. We were encouraged by our school servant-leaders to listen carefully and ask questions if we had the slightest doubt. One such visiting teacher challenged us as a class and me in particular to answer a complex question. This was how he put it.

The Bible (in Galatians 5:20) states that: "I have been crucified with Christ." If that is so, then how do you think this is possible?

He then encouraged us to go away for the rest of the one-hour period and *prayerfully* seek an answer. A whole hour on just six words!

I found a quiet spot and settled in to try to stop my usual flood of self-interested thoughts.

How could I have been crucified with Christ?

I began by looking at logic, seeking the straight edges.

In what way crucified *with* Christ?

Clearly not nailed *over* Him, or for that matter *under* Him. So, how?

In my musing, it was as if I walked around the cross to see it from all sides. That was how I came to be behind it, and that's where I found my old self.

It was an awful sight!

I was nailed as He was nailed, but in all other respects it was completely different. My hair was neatly combed and in place, my face glowed with an even tan, and I had a wide smile. I wore a crisp, white, lightly starched cotton shirt with French cuffs, my old school tie, a finely tailored Prince of Wales checked suit, and a pair of perfectly polished shoes.

It was actually revolting!

"O Lord," I cried out. "What is *that*?"

Again, it was an *almost* audible reply. "That is your old self: the *appearance* of you, the one that you still think looks pretty good. You have confessed your sins and have been forgiven. Now confess your self-sufficiency and self-approval and leave it there. Come, follow Me."

I returned to the class that day with the *beginning* of a new attitude. Thankfully, we were not asked to tell the class of our personal revelations. I'm not sure I would have known how to explain it at the time; however, *now* some twenty-six years later, I've begun to understand the entire verse:

"I have been crucified with Christ;
it is no longer
I who live, but Christ lives in me."

I like to think that it was that set-apart time that opened my heart wide enough to receive the seed of the idea we now call "outdulgence."

That clear milestone in our nine years was when, in 1979, I received a vision — one so detailed and so completely beyond my own feelings or experience at the time that I hastened to those in *servant* leadership to get their input, rather than make another presumptuous mistake! "Through insolence comes nothing but strife, but wisdom is with those who receive counsel" (Prov. 13:10).

Before I share this with you, let me please lay a little groundwork on the vision thing.

We strongly believe that God communicates. We discern these communications with *spiritual* ears and eyes that call to our hearts and minds that which *cannot be otherwise received.*

Now we are well aware that we share the same faith in Jesus Christ with other *family* members who believe, with utmost sincerity, that when "that which is perfect has come" there will be an end to such spiritual communications. These dear people quite rationally accept the Holy Scriptures as that which is perfect and, therefore, *enough.*

The last thing in the world we want to do is to contest this understanding. All we ask, if this is your view, is that you examine what we try to explain with an open spiritual mind. If the vision didn't come from God, then it is a construction assembled within my mind from exposure to ideas and/or needs that I've absorbed along the way.

Of the two, I would much prefer the vision to be "of God," especially because I have absolutely no idea where I could have been exposed to such a range of inputs. All this is vitally important because, as you will see, it is the foundation upon which outdulgence has emerged.

I received the vision during a time of prayer in the meeting area on the YWAM base in

Kailua Kona on the Big Island of Hawaii late in 1979. I had my spiral-bound notebook open in front of me and a pencil. By the time it *finished* I had covered an entire page with the illustration and the understanding.

On pages 250–51 is the order in which I received the illustration; the understanding came after the drawing was complete.

Treena and I have now lived with this communication for more than twenty-five years. At *no* time in that entire quarter century have we seen or heard or been offered by others any modification of any of its pieces, including the understanding. What has taken place is a gradual clustering of confirmation from "that which is perfect" (Scriptures) and that which is open for all to see with our *natural* eyes and ears.

We have been left with these conclusions:

- The central issue describes the role of today's church.
- The church's primary role is to be a collective witness to Jesus Christ — what He said, what He did, and what He continues to do in our individual lives today.
- Upon these truths is to be balanced the forces of true morality and social justice.

- God's heart breaks for the rich and the poor and seeks healing for them both through interaction.
- Major interaction is disrupted by a lack of trust in the ethical distribution of donations.
- God wants the church to become the wise and trustworthy steward of these donations.
- The church can (and should) develop a balanced outreach of members (selected according to their confirmed gifting) who would be sent out to achieve two goals:
  1. *To the Advantaged:* To teach to share out of abundance with others in need and to receive back from the needy the reward of their encouraged faith.
  2. *To the Disadvantaged:* To teach how to provide for their own families and communities with low-input sustainable lifestyles, so that there may be peace on all sides and an assurance that there is a provider God who loves them.

Our *servant* leaders in YWAM, being well practiced in receiving a wide variety of spiritual "leadings," looked through the

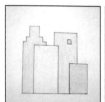

New York office buildings. One window stands out.

1

Indian mother with dying child in Calcutta

2

Barbed wire bars contact with the needy.

3

Balsa wood model with concave top

4

Ball bearing fits on top.

5

Large plank is balanced on ball bearing.

6

New York office buildings appear on one end.

7

Immediately mother and child on the other

8

The barbed wire separates the two.

9

Close-up of the wooden model with two doors

10

One door opens and man with video equipment walks to RV.

11

Man joined by a man with a pot.

12

This team sets out for New York office.

13

The other door opens and two men with agricultural equipment

14

Two men reach impoverished location.

15

The vision in all its parts

16

The city of Manhattan and one office window high up. An executive gets ready to write a check. **1**	He has "seen" the need of the poor in Calcutta. **2**	He then "sees" how his donation gets "ripped" on its way to the need. He sighs and doesn't write the check. **3**	This is a "model" church response. God's ongoing solution to those in need. **4**
The ball bearing represents Jesus, who causes everything to work together smoothly when lifted up by the church. **5**	The plank becomes perfectly balanced on Jesus. **6**	On one end those who are "rich" in blessings of all kinds. **7**	On the other end, a single human need . . . a perfect "balance" in God's eye. **8**
The barbed insinuations of the devil: "Your money won't get to the need." **9**	"My solution is with My church." **10**	"I will send 'technical' teams to those with an abundance . . . **11**	. . . and teach lifestyle benefits." **12**
"I will also send out from My church those trained to meet urgent and long-range needs." **13**	"These teams will go to the uttermost parts, sent out by consistent support from those with an abundance." **14**	"My love in My gospel will reach all those in need." **15**	"At the present time your surplus is [available] for their need, so that their abundance may also become [available] for your need, that there may be equality" (2 Cor. 8:14 HCSB). **16**

illustration and allowed that it was both clear and practical and had therefore passed the first test.

The second test was to see if it communicated.

"Write down the revelation and make it plain on tablets
so that a herald may run with it."
HABAKKUK 2:2 NIV

We were encouraged to take it on the road and to present it to both YWAM bases and the church worldwide. We did just that and lathered off another layer of our soapy reserves.

We delivered the message to the church in the USA, Canada, UK, Netherlands, France, Singapore, New Zealand, and Australia. We were well received and greatly blessed with many new friends, but to our knowledge *nobody* put the vision into practice! It failed the second test. What was clearly needed was a model — a *living* example.

It became clear that our home base in the Pacific Islands *may* have proved to be an obstacle when discussing lifestyle. We had been told on one occasion, "That's all right for you living in Hawaii. All you do is wander down to the garden and pick a banana, and no need for heating oil!"

We could "feel" the other unspoken "judgments," so we decided it was time to move to the mainland to a YWAM base in Salem, Oregon, who's leadership had enthusiastically embraced the idea — and there were no bananas!

It was at this time that I was invited by John Stott, the well-known Evangelical Anglican vicar of All Souls in Langham Place, London, England, to attend (as a *nonverbal observer*) a meeting of theologians brought together by the Lausanne Covenant to study the issue of Christian lifestyle choices in the light of the Great Commission.

I sat in silence for two weeks (surely a miracle!) listening to men and women of God from all over the world drafting a paper on lifestyle. The event was called "The Hoddeston Conference 1980." At the end of the second week, the working members had ratified a document of some fourteen pages, with elaborate argument well undergirded with Scripture.

"Graham, over here please." It was John Stott, and he wanted *me!* "The BBC World Service wants to do a small piece about our meetings here," he explained in his slightly offhand manner.

"That's good," I replied, somewhat mystified as to why he should tell me.

"I want you to go down and do the interview," he explained.

"But John, I . . . er . . . you said I was to be a *silent* observer."

"Well, that was during the drafting. You are not a theologian, but you're a communicator. Most theologians aren't communicators, especially in four minutes or less," he added with a wry smile.

"But John, fourteen pages in four minutes. I don't think I could do it," I protested.

"Do you believe the Bible?" he asked.

"Well, yes," I replied cautiously.

". . . where it says that the mouths of His witnesses would be filled as they stood before the magistrates." He was now quite stern.

"You mean you want me to go on the BBC *World* Service and just open my mouth and believe that God will fill it?"

"Precisely." He was moving off to catch up with a fellow theologian from East Africa.

I decided to do *exactly* what he had suggested, more out of a rebellious attitude than by faith. How could he suggest such a thing? What a risk for him to take with *me*!

I arrived at the BBC in London and was shown into a tiny studio with a large microphone and the smaller-than-life interviewer.

"Hello, Graham," he beamed from ear to ear. "My mum and I used to watch your show together," he explained as he pumped my hand and clapped me on the back like an old friend.

I was immediately grateful to have such a warm reception because I simply didn't have a clue what I would say. In fact, I'd decided not to even work out a fall-back position in case God decided *not* to fill my mouth.

"When the red light comes on, we'll be live, worldwide. Isn't this fun?" he observed with great enthusiasm.

I wanted to open my mouth, wide.

"This is the BBC Worldwide Service. We have in the studio tonight Graham Kerr [he pronounced my name *cur,* not *care*]. He's been with *God* [heavy emphasis here] for the past two weeks. So, what's God saying?" His delivery was measured, his accent less northern, his tone both bored and skeptical. I opened my very dry mouth, closed it, and swallowed.

Now, I've confessed to having had a vision on a previous occasion and, therefore, having just a tiny seed of faith to apply to this urgent need.

I *saw* an army boot crashing into the

gravel of a parade ground and then another. Then I saw a drill sergeant standing in front of the squad shouting, "By the left, quick march!"

Not knowing where it was going, I opened my mouth again. "Were you ever in the Army?" I asked.

"Yes," he replied.

"Did anyone ever say *by the left, quick march?*"

"Yes . . . hmm." He was looking a little nervous.

"What foot did you step off with?" I was getting some understanding.

"The left." He was now ill at ease and ready to pull the switch where they apologize for an interruption to the program.

"Exactly." It was I who now beamed with relief.

"You mean *God* [he drew out that name again] said, 'By the left, quick march'?"

"Yes, in a manner of speaking," I replied quickly. "You see, the left foot is the gospel message — the good news that we can find forgiveness for causing others pain because Jesus Christ died in our place so that we could begin a new life here *and* spend an eternity with Him.

"The right foot," I hurried on in order to get both feet in without interruption, "The right foot is social justice — the *provisions* that are necessary so that mankind can provide for their own family security and well-being and to believe that there is a God who loves them and provides for them.

"The problem we face today as Christians," I went on, "is that various traditions have set off with different feet and then dragged the other foot along like a prosthetic behind them and *that*" — it was now my time for heavy emphasis — "and *that* is why the modern church appears to be so inconsistent and uncoordinated." I sat back to see if he'd got it.

He had!

We continued to chat in a much more friendly way for the balance of the four minutes.

I learned much later that in the late 1800s a philosopher by the name of C. E. Leesing had introduced this inconsistency by suggesting that there was a "great ugly chasm" in the Christian life that could not be bridged. On the one side were the "eternal" truths for which there were no *factual* support — only faith. And on the other side were indeed all that could be factually measured.

In other words, he had driven a wedge of words into the solid block of truth that God does *in fact* (measurably so) provide both salvation and day-to-day provision, and when both are present, there is abundant evidence in support of His faithfulness and grace.

Our belief is that when outdulgence is applied within the modern church, it will be seen as a clear example of the *one great commandment* upon which depends all the law and all the prophets.

"He said to him, 'Love the Lord your God
with all your heart, with all your soul,
and with all your mind.
This is the greatest and most
important commandment.
The second is like it:
Love your neighbor as yourself.'"
MATTHEW 22:37–39 HCSB

CHAPTER TWENTY-EIGHT: TACOMA

"Judge not that you be not judged."
Oh, how true this saying of Jesus.
Thus it seems when you're one,
you both have to suffer His censure.

Greatly buoyed by my "apparent" willingness to trust God to fill my mouth, I returned to the United States and the Oregon YWAM base where we had built our first *smaller* house and purchased our truly *unloaded* car — a 1979 Citation, with no air-conditioning, no radio, and not even a clock. We did get a friend to install a sunshine roof, but he got it sufficiently off-center to be noticed.

I was clearly being influenced by fourteen *closely typed* pages of theology and had entered into a period of legalism in which anyone who did anything or who owned anything or wore anything that exceeded what we did or owned or wore was in borderline idolatry.

Writing about this period in our lives isn't easy because it's so obviously tragic and misguided, and yet, for all that, it seems to be a rite of passage, undergone by many.

It is because of this that I'm more than willing to spend some time wallowing in my mistakes, on the chance that I may help *anyone* avoid becoming such an appalling witness.

I don't want to disagree with my darling; however, he seemed very like a lot of churchy people I knew! This is NOT judgmental. It's the truth! So, I really didn't notice his "appalling witness." I just knew there was a little criticism going on in his life, but that was God's job to correct, not mine, and I was in no doubt that He would. (I just didn't realize I was going to have to suffer with him!) However, I did learn a lot about things I would never have learned elsewhere. Nothing is ever wasted with Him. Isn't that a comforting truth?

What was happening, I can now see more clearly, was a merger of several of my well-established behavior characteristics that included my search for logical straight edges, my hang-up with appearances, and my enormous need to be accepted by my fellow Christians as a *servant* rather than a *celebrity*.

It is perfectly obvious to anyone, Christian or non-Christian alike, that the world's present state of distress is a direct consequence of noncompliance. In the medical field, *noncompliance* could mean what happens when you don't take your medications. In the spiritual realm, it almost always means when Christians choose not to follow a few quite clear and explicit *commandments.*

One estimate suggests that two-thirds of everything that can be owned on this planet is owned by those who at least claim to be "Christian." Back in 1980, I began to swallow these statistics wholesale. I and my fellow Christians had been commanded to love God, the poor, our neighbors, each other, and even our enemies, and to follow up this love with truly practical examples of generosity, *even if that meant personal sacrifice.* We decided to set off on that road less traveled, to squeeze through the "eye of the needle," and to carry on where the rich, young ruler had left off.

Because the object of all this would be the presentation of the gospel and the provision of *sacrificial* resources, we were convinced that the church needed only to be awakened in order to reengage with *both feet* the completion of the Great Commission.

But how to awaken the church? We had

tried to reach out, but nobody had apparently *seen* what it could mean.

We were back to the need for a model.

In 1980, we were invited to visit the YWAM base in Tacoma, Washington, a few hundred miles north of Salem, Oregon. It was a typically gray winter day, and a keen wind was driving the sulfurous pulp aromas over the city from Commencement Bay. Cold, damp, smelly — not a good day to visit. We took the road leading to the Stadium High School from the city center and, glancing to the left, saw a huge redbrick edifice with its black-framed notice board: First Presbyterian Church of Tacoma.

"I bet there's a bunch of frozen chosen in there." I laughed at my own poor judgment, and then I lost control of the car, skidding off the wet roadway onto the sidewalk.

"What's going on!" cried Treena.

"I don't know. The wheel just wrenched out of my hand." I was quite shaken.

"Let's pray," I suggested because somehow the need was perfectly obvious with our car half on and half off the roadway!

Once again, came that nearly audible voice, but this time not so soft. "Don't you dare speak about *any* part of my church like that."

And then followed an explicit command. "You are to attend that church."

See, once you are one, you are one. I was not thrilled at this prospect, I can tell you! However, I had to be who God had made me with some added refinement. I realized I couldn't go dancing round the church. I would give them all a heart attack. I was told by a certain lady that it wasn't done to hug men in their church. About two weeks after this remark, though, she asked forgiveness and told me that God had told her she was jealous, and why didn't she give people holy hugs. Bless her, I only hugged our friends after that though. I also got to pray for people who cried when I prayed because they had never been prayed for before! I had a great friend who loved the Lord with all her heart. It was through her I realized that not everyone had to speak in tongues to love God. There were always lessons to learn, and the church truly accepted us as we accepted them. For eight years God had us there, both of us learning so much as a result of critical attitudes!

We hadn't even decided to live in Tacoma, let alone worship at an old, big church with a black-framed notice board on a windy, wet, smelly corner!

But the decision was made for us, so we obeyed. We moved from our small home in Oregon to a very small apartment in the windy, wet, and *occasionally* smelly city, and we stayed there for eight years. We spent those eight years as members of the First Presbyterian Church, the very congregation that I had accused of being "frozen."

It was within this part of the body of Christ that we developed a model that would provide an example for the rest of the Christian world.

Chapter Twenty-Nine: The Creative Lifestyle Group

"Outdulgence" really started here,
with these Tacoma friends.
The Creative Lifestyle Group
still is an absolute God-send.

We were to work on the model from 1981 to 1987. During this period, we became servant-leaders of "Operation LORD" (long-range development). We built and operated the Creative Lifestyle Center, which displayed and taught lifestyle issues. I was licensed by the Assemblies of God as a pastor and ordained as a Presbyterian elder.

The Lord had us both growing in individual ways. My teaching opportunity started in YWAM and was restarted here in the Presbyterian church and became my new career, sending me to Singapore, New Zealand, Australia, Canada, England, and much of the United States — another blessing from my Lord!

So many irons in the fire and so many traditions for an early Anglican who had been baptized in the Church of the Brethren!

Most of our work was a well-intentioned application of the "vision" received back in Hawaii. We had come to understand that God was equally compassionate about both the poor and the rich, and, therefore, we could attempt through the church to reach out to both.

Now, all of this would have been fine had it not been for one major issue that I have eventually come to call *digital evangelism*.

From the earliest days of the Christian church, there have been many core movements that have continued to declare the goal of world evangelism. Its cornerstone argument was that, when once every tribe and people group had heard the gospel, then the end would come.

An end to what? Well, to those who endured all kinds of pain and persecution, it meant an end to the rule of evil and the start of God's kingdom. For those who believed, this was the best of good news and worthy of much effort.

Of course, those who didn't share the Christian faith were not exactly pleased about the prospect of the sudden termination of their apparent freedom. However, most unbelievers were skeptical enough to dismiss the idea of "completion" along with all the rest of the "story." This did not (and does not) deter evangelical Christians from continuing to plan the way to completion.

It was this exercise of logic that got me into what became a counterfeit commission — one that was focused upon *numbers* rather than *people*.

The great evangelical conference in Edinborough, Scotland, had declared in 1888 that, with a determined working together of the major denominations present, the commission could be completed by 1900. The Lausanne Evangelical Covenant took up the cause, yet pursued it with no fixed date. The U.S. Center for World Missions continues to embrace a wide variety of initiatives and to show how reaching the entire world is within our grasp.

Numbers — when we had reached *enough* then evil was *over!*

For me, it became a numbers game. I set up an elaborate global system that applied the Operation LORD vision to the established local church. Bingo! I could prove not only the world could be reached, but how! And by 2011.

Of course, I wasn't alone. So compelling is the idea of a new heaven and a new earth (especially to those who find the present earth unacceptable), that evangelical Christianity is constantly exploring both the how and the when of completion. My problem was that I had become so judgmental, so critical of the loss of values, so distressed at the failure to meet so many urgent deeds, that I just wanted the *failure* to *stop!*

Notice that what I was lacking was *love.* I was wanting an end to sin more than the enormous blessing of life for each and every *digit* of the *numbers* who made up my digital evangelical effort.

I can see it now — I couldn't see it then. If you give your body to be burned and have not love, it profits you *nothing.*

It would profit nothing;
Should one's body burn,
In martyrdom, and one not love.
Clearly these words state
That loveless sacrifice is death.
Do not the words request
Compassion without compromise?
The Word with us in partnership,
While suffering a cup to sip,
Does say — to pray, to go, to give,
Yet, oneself will gain pure joy
As true love meets the untold
Pain, of hurting peoples.

To care, to love, to weep
With those who weep,
Brings joy, with peace
That passes every understanding.

We've explained this, as best as we can, in order to expose the reason why so much apparent logic, based upon so much scriptural truth, can lead nowhere — well, almost nowhere, *because God always protects His seed.*

My *interview* with the senior pastor of the First Presbyterian Church of Tacoma, Dr. Albert Lindsay, didn't go well. Dr. Lindsay was a stern, biblical teacher whose radio broadcasts had been a tremendous blessing to many. He was held in high regard by the congregation. I wanted his blessing to begin a Creative Lifestyle group within the church, a group that would explore the idea that would become outdulgence.

Dr. Lindsay took me out to see a small garden with flagstone paths in the church grounds.

"There now," he said as he waved his hand around the entire area, "can you see a spare piece of ground unplanted?"

"No, Dr. Lindsay, I can't," I replied.

"Precisely." He had made his point. There

was no room in the church for another pro-gram, and while he remained senior pastor, that was that!

Later, following his retirement, I tried again. Some of the earlier plantings had been uprooted, and I got my chance.

We met each Sunday in the Gold Room, as part of the Sunday school class that met in the building often set aside for funerals. We called ourselves a "Creative Lifestyles Group," but our subject was "Counting the Cost of Commitment." The basic idea was to estimate what might happen to us if we made a lifestyle commitment to complete (as God would lead) the Great Commission. We understood that it would be a shame if we were to begin something and then not com-plete it. We had the normal thirteen-week teaching "cycle," so we divided the time between the two of us and began to explore how we might collectively become a *model*. The basic idea attracted an extraordinary group, with several very experienced elders who remain to this day a great encourage-ment to us both.

For several years, Treena and I have be-come aware of the fact that we saw things differently. It wasn't just the male/female vantage point — it went way beyond the normal. We were what I used to order at the Savoy Hotel River Restaurant where the roast beef was carved at the tableside: "I'll have an in and out cut, please." The chef de range would then carve a slice from the dark, crusted, salty exterior, and another from the deep pink interior.

Treena was the inside, the deeper, emotionally charged issues. And I was the outside — the obvious practical applications of logic and appearance! We knew enough by that time that, if we were to focus on the exterior applications, we would quickly develop yet another set of legalisms. We needed to get in touch with the inner motives, issues that needed to be a more consistent support to the so often hard-to-change outer habits.

Of course, by this time I had read 2 Timothy 2:15: "Be diligent to present yourself approved to God, a worker who doesn't need to be ashamed, correctly teaching the word of truth" (HCSB). Being Treena, who still had some hang-ups, I worked extra hard to make sure I would be approved by God and by those Christian critics whom I feared might be just waiting to pounce!

I love teaching. I love to help other people change and discover Jesus as their friend. I definitely have felt the call of God in this area. I am enabled by Him to be transparent about my own needs and healings; this helps others to accept their own problems and realize they aren't alone. The Lord kept opening the doors for me to teach, until I had to stop, once more, to serve my Graham.

Treena taught from her long experience as a communicator, both as an actress and a television producer. Her past media expertise converged with her new spiritual life, and she received considerable revelation on what she described as *hearing and listening*.

She went on to describe for all of us what might be involved should we decide to commit to *loving* others *unconditionally*. Treena got deeper when she suggested that our *criticism* of each other prevented this unconditional love we might desire, and that it often had its roots in *rejection*. She led us all in a rejection of rejection and then to the building of a strong desire to *restore relationships* that we might never have thought could be healed.

Following our six weeks of internal healing, I took over what was by then a pretty well-ploughed field (with several harrowing experiences).

We looked at the *race* set before us and the six key words we needed to somehow understand on an individual basis. These were

humility, compassion, abundance, contentment, enjoyment, and endurance. We then
went on to explore the six words in groups
of two.

Humility and *Compassion* led us to check
out our blessings and our personal fruitfulness, then consider how we might restore
relationships, better use time, and measure
our personal sphere of influence (PSI).

Abundance and *Contentment* caused us to
assess what we actually had available. We
did an exercise in financial planning and we
discussed motivational drift — when we had
somehow gotten off track and missed God's
purposes for our lives.

Enjoyment and *Endurance*. We prioritized
our levels of enjoyment and assessed our
past experiences with huge "hurdles" that
seemed impossible to clear, and yet, by
God's grace, we overcame.

Finally, we spent a good deal of time looking once again at our lifestyle and considering past fruitfulness (or otherwise) and future choices. We had agreed that, during the
class duration, we would individually, without telling one another, come to the point of
decision on commitment. We would commit
first to the Lord and then to whatever work
He might direct us.

By the end of the series, every one of us

(twenty-eight in all) had made a commitment. Embedded in that commitment was a promise to try to find fifty cents per day of individual habit change and to take that sum and give it to the savings account set up in the church to handle this new money. We agreed not to discuss the amount of money we were giving — only the steps taken to change a habit.

When the class was over, we agreed to send two of the college-age Sunday school participants to Brazil to spy out the land. We had *felt* as a group that Brazil was somewhere we needed to serve.

That was in 1982. I'm delighted to report that one of the young men sent out, Mark Barnes, did report back and was officially sent out *unto a specific purpose* in Brazil, where he serves to this day with his Brazilian wife Iris, *twenty-three years later,* and still counts several of our class members as his faithful supporters.

It was during this time that I was to learn several vitally important lessons:

- The Great Commission is about loving *people,* one person at a time. Assessing them as percentages for programmatic purposes doesn't add up to love, and it *can* mean manipulation for selfish ambition, which is of no use whatsoever.

- It's much better to choose to: "Do a small thing and to do it well, until it's done."
- It's much better to consistently *lean into* something that needs to be changed than to push or pull, shout or dictate. Uproar is what the media loves to report. Humility is what God loves to observe.

What I have learned through the teaching experience is that one needs to be transparent at the same time as listening to oneself and the Holy Spirit. I remember quite early on in my ministry I heard God say, "Treena, that's a lie." I stopped speaking and argued, "But, Lord, it was only an exaggeration." "An exaggeration is a lie!" Right then and there He had me tell the people that I was a liar! The congregation gasped. I shall never forget the sound. Then I explained to them my lesson from the Lord, that an exaggeration is a lie!

This has happened in different ways, many times. I have to listen and learn while I speak. Teaching can always be a school of learning for the teacher, and how!

We had obeyed, when half on the roadway

and half on the sidewalk. We had moved to a cold, wet, occasionally smelly city (that we had come to love), and we had learned how to love in the company of God's "frozen chosen." When pride raises an ugly, painful bruise, apply ice — it helps!

CHAPTER THIRTY:
MOTIVATIONAL DRIFT

How many times are we sure that we're right,
and everything points to the factual?
How many times have we drifted off course,
to be saved by a personal angel?
Sometimes we go really off track, led by
an inspiration that really was not!
The devil is always waiting to make everything
look like it is, when it's not!

To explain what happened next, we need to go back a few years to our sailing adventure in 1973, before we ran aground in the Chesapeake.

In 1973, on our way north up the Atlantic coast of the United States, we chose to go direct from Manhasset Bay, just north of New York City, to Newport, Rhode Island. It was a fine summer's day, without a cloud in either the sky or the forecast. I drew a straight line from bay to port, with no course changes, no reefs or shoals or headlands — just plain motoring, a ho-hum trip for us after all the blue water challenges . . . or so we thought.

The day continued as planned, straight up the pencil line with no problems. But something was going on that we had not encountered in the Mediterranean or the Caribbean. The weather was misting toward a fog. They have very few fogs down south, and beneath us a strong tide was running, again mostly unnoticed. I had allowed for neither. Our heading remained true to the pencil line.

The fog rolled in; the wind picked up. We turned on the radar and began looking out for navigation buoys. On the deck, we heard a soft gong on our port side. "Buoy to port," I cried down to our friend Tin Tin, who manned the radar. "I have it," he shouted. "Still right on track."

The miles wound on, and buoys of various types drifted past. We held our course heading as we closed on Newport.

Our daughter, Tessa, was up forward in the bow as an added lookout. Tin Tin was on radar and I was at the wheel. The fog was really thick, the sea up to a three-foot chop.

"We should be entering the harbor area now." Tin Tin was matching up the radar with his copy of the chart (this was *obviously* before GPS).

"Rocks to starboard!" Tessa yelled. I spun the wheel hard to port as we lurched through the waves.

"What's going on?" Treena poked her head over the companionway.

"We seem to be lost," I replied, trying to sound both calm and in control and feeling neither.

And there we stopped, slopping about in the seaway, trying to make sense of the chart and the radar. It looked as if we had arrived, *but we hadn't!*

We heard it before we saw it: the putt-putt-putt of a smaller diesel and then abruptly a twenty-eight-foot blue sailboat swept past us within a dozen feet or so.

I swallowed my pride in owning a seventy-one-foot ocean racing ketch and hailed the twenty-eight-footer. "Ahoy, er . . ." — I strained to see her name — "er . . . Blue Angel," I shouted.

The putt-putts quietened, and the boat slowed and turned toward us.

"Aaarh," barked the bearded skipper.

"We appear to be lost." This was not easy to admit publicly! "Are you going to New-port?" I asked. He was now almost along-side, and I was able to look down into his cockpit.

"Aaarh." His vocabulary was limited, but

his inflection gave me enough confidence.

"Can I follow you?" Surely this was the ultimate act of humility for a seasoned, very British blue-water yachtsman to propose to a bearded Yankee sailor who might have been descended from John Paul Jones for all I knew.

"A-aaarh," he agreed and putt-putted off into the fog, with me close astern like his enormous dinghy.

We later discovered that the tides, the wind, and the sea had swept us sideways even while we kept on the same northern heading. The buoys we had heard we hadn't even *seen*. The numbers were wrong, and some of the ones that had bells should have moaned! The bay we had entered was seven miles off course. We had been heading straight for the rocks while remaining on course and using radar.

Is it like that in our spiritual lives? Does everything appear to be on track and yet isn't?

We now call this *motivational drift,* and it was about to take us on a fifteen-year detour.

CHAPTER THIRTY-ONE:
CASH FLOW
OR MUDSLIDE

When does one learn to pray and ask God?
How long does it take us to learn?
We make our mistakes, we pick ourselves up,
Then do the same things over again.

The Sisters of Providence are a Roman Catholic order that has always ministered to the sick, especially on the West Coast. Exactly how they came to know about us is unknown, but those who made contact were among their Protestant administrators. They were attracted to our Display Center, the one we were busily building in order to attract and inform Christians who wanted to expand upon the model we had developed at First Pres in Tacoma.

"Would you consider making a series of videos for our patients?" they asked. "You see, we have a problem with postoperative care. We give them very careful surgical remedies for their heart health, but when they go home — well, they don't stick with the program," explained our Protestant friend. Now to some degree this was "off track," and yet it *was* helping people within a Christian context, and we needed the cash flow in those early ministry days. If we had stopped to study the vision (see pp. 250–51), we would have slowed down enough to at least pray.

We did neither. All we could see was the pencil line running north. We just didn't see the tidal effect or the slight mistiness in the air. We agreed to make this series with an extremely talented filmmaker, Michael Lienau of Global Net News. We called it the "Double Benefit" and built into it our understanding of *being well enough to serve others*. At least *something* of our ministry would be included!

I thought this was all very nice; however, it seemed to be more like a salve for the guilt I felt. Giving money was always the easy way. When we were poor, then giving was a selfless act. But fifty cents a day? That didn't seem to be very much of a sacrifice. Now, to make a video, yes! That would be fun and could help people get well. I was all for it.

I would be doing something I loved to do and helping others in the little skits and the ques-

tions I would ask. Well, it certainly seemed to make more sense to me, and I enjoyed the acting parts. It seemed so right for our ministry and fun to do — but once again, as Graham said, we didn't pray!

It took us about a year to do the research, production, and postproduction. It was fun, informative, and not overly expensive when we looked at the nine half-hour "shows." Unfortunately it got lost in the fog of an internal crisis in which the very loving Mother Superior left to marry a local priest! We were paid, life went on, and the videos went unseen, *but we had been dragged off course.*

Shortly after this brush with the media, we were contacted by the now-famous Aaron Brown (CNN), who was at that time a local associate anchor in Seattle. He was interested in our work as a part of "whatever happened to such-and-such a celebrity" series. He was late arriving at our small corner house on Puget Sound Road in Tacoma. "I drove past three times," Aaron explained his lateness. "I couldn't believe you'd live in a house like this." He waved his hand at our modest dwelling.

Aaron's comment lay there in my heart like parsley seed. I'm told that parsley is so hard to germinate that a gardener once said,

"It goes down to its devil seven times before it comes up." His words certainly went somewhere before they helped to nudge us way off course.

We were well into 1987 when Treena had her stroke. I got the news at the Display Center and rushed over to St. Joseph's Hospital, thumping the steering wheel, crying out, "Why, why, why, God?" As if I didn't know!

Back in 1978, immediately prior to joining Youth With A Mission, Treena and I had had what we now call "The Battle of the Bologna." She finally got fed up with my gastronomic legalisms and flung slices of bologna sausage all over the kitchen to let me know that enough was enough!

Bologna flew, flew, flew.
Fury made this rare debut.
"Can't eat this. Can't eat that."
Another piece graced this act
As anger grew; more slices flew,
Landing at Gra's feet, on cue.
Soon they were done, so cupboards next
Were emptied in the garbage bin.
I punctuated each item flung with "FINE!"
First one, then two, then three with
"There-is-nothing-left-to-eat-with-you."
"OK, OK, you have your way. I'll eat mine."

I had won, or so I thought; it wasn't true.
But it was fine, fine, fine — until!

I got the message and began a two-menu lifestyle. I stuck with my broccoli, brewer's yeast, and bran flakes (almost everything began with a "b" and was good for the bowels!). Treena, our son Andy, our daughter Kareena, and my mother Mardi ate from another, more classic menu.

Nine years of unwise eating sponsored by her rebellion to my too-wise eating was the cause of her stroke, or had at least contributed. What appeared to be a massive 80 percent blockage of the carotid artery on one test, turned out to be only 20 percent on another. I put the difference down to prayer. Treena put it down *completely* and denied it had ever happened, even in the face of an opinion shared by two neurosurgeons!

Yes, well. I didn't believe it. I didn't want people to think I was a hypochondriac. I believed that it was my arm, which I had strained, and they were wrong! Remember the poem on page 192 about being the best and never complaining? My parents' comments had truly taken root. This shows how careful we need to be when we speak to our children. I wish I had realized this when I was bringing up my children. You mean I wasn't perfect either?

Later in 1987, we returned to Hawaii to take a special Leadership Training School with a substantial part of the "old guard" who had joined YWAM in its very early days. It was during this rather intense school at the University of the Nations campus that Treena had her heart attack.

Both of these events are interesting in retrospect because both were initially assessed as "life threatening," and yet within weeks of each, she was apparently healed without any need for surgical intervention. They were interesting because what I had been saying publicly since 1975 at Cornell and elsewhere, including "The Double Benefit," was the way that I was living, but not the way we lived as a family. I'm inclined to consider both of Treena's events as wake-up calls. *Whatever is spoken in public should be lived in private.* My theology doesn't stretch far enough to include Treena's stroke and heart attack as initiated by God, but my *feelings* about the whole deal certainly embraces the idea that "whatsoever you sow, so shall you reap." Or, in other words, the choices we make can add up to *allowable* consequences.

My understanding was that God was dealing with my rebellion and denial because of Graham's legalisms. However, two wrongs can never make a right, and in my case, they definitely didn't. Such a waste of money to disobey! I promised the Lord that, in the future, I would learn to trust Him through Graham.

The Lord gave me a Scripture during this time which changed my attitude about accepting news I didn't want to hear. Second Corinthians 12:9 (HCSB): "Therefore, I will most gladly boast all the more about my weaknesses, so that Christ's power may reside in me." WOW (wonder of wonders)! To have the power of Christ dwell in me, as at no other time, because of my weaknesses! Now I had a real reason not to sidestep the issue. I could boast in His power that resided in me, rather than live in denial. This Scripture has helped me in so many ways!

Following the heart attack, Treena and I found ourselves in agreement about our joint selection of lifestyle. Treena had seen how ill I had looked in the air ambulance as we had "bumped" our way to Honolulu and intensive care. I had seen how ill she *was* and had committed to stop being so legalistic. At the same time, Treena was promising herself to do what I had said. We met somewhere in the middle with a mutual resolve to, as John of the Cross put it, "If you love someone you do them good, and the good you do them you do with the best in your nature."

It was at that extreme time of need that I *received the idea* of T.A.C.T. (taste, aroma, color, texture) that would eventually become "The Food Preference Sheet" (see www .grahamkerr.com). Literally within days we were in full agreement and in the midst of a radical and wonderful *upgrade* in our enjoyment of extremely healthy food. Treena had been given a three-month opportunity to reduce her 365 cholesterol before an assessment was made of her future medical needs. Within one month her cholesterol had dropped 125 points, and we were well on the way to being well. Then the fog descended — suddenly!

Bruce Reynolds had called from New Zealand. "Graham, we'd like you to make a series of videos about New Zealand for the Japanese tourist market." It would be summer in New Zealand and winter in our chilly, windy, wet, and sometimes-smelly Tacoma — and then there was the ever-present issue of cash flow.

We felt good about it because we could include our *new* experience with food and healing. It followed the pencil line track, but we were now *unable* to see the numbers on the buoys and were trusting the "radar of our feelings." We did pray, but also, in my search for logical straight edges, I called Wilbur Freifeld, my one-time New York lawyer/agent. What did he think? "You need to make a series of thirteen twenty-four-minute videos so that they can be used on television as well. Oh, and make them on Beta-cam, so they are broadcast quality!" The buoy that *clanged* should have moaned, and had we seen the number, we would have changed course!

I felt this was the end — that I might fall back into my old dominating ways before Jesus. I could feel the rebellion starting to rise. THIS was our new life, NOT television! I was full of dread. Not television again, PLEASE. These were my prayers as the elders prayed theirs. But His will was to be another learning curve!

This time we took the idea to our servant leaders because neither of us wanted to go back on television. Within YWAM at that time was a teaching on the "Mind Molders," an extremely powerful and logical and passionately proclaimed idea that cultures were molded by seven basic influences, one of which was the media. Another, for example, was politics.

Christians, it was argued, should be actively involved in each of these fields of human endeavor in order to spread morality, justice, and good lifestyle ethics on the broadest possible "playing field" and not be forced into a defensive posture within church walls. This teaching was very clear, and it made sense, provided that it didn't lead to compromise.

"No one lights a lamp and puts it
under a basket,
but rather on a lampstand, and it gives light
for all who are in the house."
MATTHEW 5:15 HCSB

Our leaders prayed for us and were delighted to see this example of two media-minded molders returning to their place of influence. Neither they nor we chose to review the idea in the light of the Operation LORD vision. We agreed and ploughed on into the fog.

We made the first thirteen episodes of *Simply Marvelous* with a great crew that became dear friends. New Zealand was as beautiful as ever and only upstaged by its people. But the program, like the "Double Benefit," didn't sell. Our pal Wilbur said that stations needed more than thirteen — at least thirty-nine. So Reynolds obtained funding from a Christian foundation, and another twenty-six were made in the British Isles.

They didn't sell!

We were now way off track and getting close to some hard edges of reality. The sea of complications resulting from failed expectation was rising. We were lost, and I didn't feel calm or in control. All I felt was responsible and obligated to somehow — *anyhow* — put it all right!

I wanted to pay back all the money spent, somehow, but this was impossible. We had very little money left. We had to ask forgiveness and try somehow to put things right and get out of television and go back to full-time ministry. I knew things were going to go from bad to worse, and they did! We and they must have hurt many good Christians by the time all the lessons were finished. Trust in God, not in man!

It was at this time that Reynolds Film Company was purchased by an enterprising group that called themselves West 175, and it was they who came up with an answer. "We'll make a genuinely long series of 170 episodes and create the renewed marketplace for your name and, therefore, for *Simply Marvelous!*"

In an effort to get into any kind of port where we might see our Christian supporters recompensed, we finally agreed. We signed a five-year agreement, to end on my sixtieth birthday in January 1994, to make a series that eventually played every day for several years on the Discovery Channel called *Graham Kerr.*

We moved from our "simple pad" in Tacoma to a lakeside condominium in Kirkland (which we called "yuppie heaven"). We exchanged our simple car for a Camry station wagon. We exchanged our ministry in YWAM for one as mind-molders-in-the-media. We exchanged our place in the pew in First Pres Tacoma for a more entertaining seat in a large Pentecostal church in Bothell. It looked like an *upgrade;* we were gathering the stuff that gave us the right appearance as celebrities. There were manufactured lights everywhere, but *we were hurting badly!*

We wanted to include these tough times for a specific purpose. We wanted to show what happens when, for whatever "good" and apparently "rational"' reason, we choose to leave the track less traveled for the broader highway that seems to lead to a swifter resolution of an immediate problem. The out-

Graham and Treena in New Zealand making "Simply Marvelous." Who says the other person's grass isn't always greener? This was near ChristChurch in the South Island.

come may, in fact, be worse than the initial predicament. In other words, if you can't get out of a hole, stop digging!

I strongly suspect that what we needed to do was to compare *all* these offers with the one "vision" we had received and to pray to receive any kind of release from this "approved" direction. Had we done this we would never have found ourselves in court with our lawyer shouting "ROCKS!" Our legal battles serve no useful purpose in understanding the progress of outdulgence, other than to underline our total indebtedness to the system. After six years of media

293

wilderness, we were almost five hundred thousand dollars in debt. How's that for cash flow — or was it a mudslide?

CHAPTER THIRTY-TWO:
NOTHING IS
EVER WASTED

*No bad mistakes, no deeds of fools, no bad
decisions wasted.
God turned all things His way,
once we understood we'd drifted!*

"Putt-putt-putt." We had heard it before we
saw it — the "Blue Angel" with its bearded
captain who had led us into port. Wendell
Wilkes had no beard and was considerably
more articulate than our previous nautical
St. Bernard. He also had a plan that was
able to get us into a safe port, and this time
everybody prayed *hard*.

*I should confess that my prayers were not
especially deep because once more I didn't
really trust that this was right. Even after we
prayed, I still had a check in my spirit! I wish I
had listened to that still, small voice, but logic
took over. Yes, even women experience logic
at times! We were in debt, and there seemed*

no other way. Wendell was a very nice man, another Christian, and this time appeared to know what he was doing. Also, I thought, this could be God's answer. There was a great enthusiasm, both within Wendell's company and within our hearts. Once more, we entered the fray together. Once more we would try to fight our way upstream.

We would make another long series — this time 130 episodes to be called *The Gathering Place.* The series would combine good food with good science and, therefore, meet the ever-increasing need for a caring media that might somehow offset the destructive effects of some types of advertising and programming.

We made the series between January 1995, when we began its worldwide research, and 2000 when the last episode was recorded. Unlike the last two media attempts, this one did sell — *just!* (Please see p. 343 for a "Stop Press" announcement about this series, now on DVD.)

To some degree everyone who had been involved in our return to the media had been impressed or influenced by the original success of the *Galloping Gourmet* and were looking for lightning to strike a second time. The problem, as I see it now, is that while I appeared to be able to communicate as well (or better, *some* would say), my script was the issue. In the *Galloping Gourmet* I would throw large lumps of meat into a great deal of clarified butter, then flambé it in good cognac and quench the flames with double cream. For those antics I was named "The High Priest of Hedonism," which, if one examines the rating of that time (in the early 1970s), was exactly what people wanted to see. We actually sold eleven million hard-backed cookbooks at that time, which sort of proves my point on acceptance.

Now please flip the coin onto its other side. As the "new" Graham Kerr (who had "found God," as the media chooses to describe Christian faith), I would throw no more than three and a half ounces of "light" meat into a half teaspoon of olive oil and garnish it with a colorful horde of fresh vegetables. For these efforts I was named "The Cook Who Cares." If you choose to examine the ratings of these shows (albeit in a totally overwhelmed marketplace of a hundred or so channels), you will find that, even though the audience may need it (67 percent overweight or obese), they don't necessarily want to watch it.

So much for *mind-molders* of a culture, especially when proposing that the culture reverse course! As I review our fifteen-year detour, I cannot call it all loss because during that time I was able to learn a great deal and see my beloved Treena return to good health. However, I can easily see how I abdicated my position as a simple witness as I chased after the illusive influence of a celebrity in search of cash flow.

Once you have set your hand to the plough, never look back (see Luke 9:62).

How easy it would be to settle into a whole new chapter and examine the *what-ifs* of our fifteen-year detour. What might have happened to the creative lifestyle model in the local church, and what might have happened to the Display Center if the *media* had not intervened? And yet there is no fruit in such conjecture because it didn't happen, and, therefore, it cannot instruct, and its only fruit is guilt or recrimination, so I'll plough on to another well-known verse.

"All things work together for good
to those who love God, to those who are
the called according to His purpose."
ROMANS 8:28 NKJV

So since *things* did actually take place in those fifteen years, how could they become *good?*

In that fifteen-year period Treena and I made 1,012 individual episodes for many different purposes. Some were for hospitals, others for the American Heart Association, for the public media, and also for the National Cancer Institute. Every single episode explored how food contributed to better health. During those fifteen years I entered into a whole range of relationships with men and women of science and their institutions. Many became good friends; they all gave us their best advice unselfishly and for the common good.

During those fifteen years, I read more than four hundred scientific papers on human nutrition. Most of them were from conservative Western medical practice, but some edged into the "new" fields of alternatives that had been well proven.

During those fifteen years I served as the first visiting professor at the Culinary Institute of America, where I also "performed" as part of their Great Chefs program. Later I lectured at Johnson Wales University, where I received an Honorary Doctorate in Culinary Nutrition. During this period I was inducted into the American Academy of Chefs Hall of Fame (again in an honorary capacity), received the title of Diplomat from the American Culinary Federation, and an honorary life membership in the American Dietetic Association. To cap it all off, I won the Julia Child Cookbook award (for "diet-related" books).

During those fifteen years I also wrote eight books and was therefore obligated to "strut my stuff" on all kinds of national and local television shows, radio, and personal appearances. The consistent element of all this activity was the celebrity factor. *Celebrity* has been defined as being well known for being well known. It is not so much a matter of being known for a specific action as being *known*. And being *known* can be as simple as getting media attention on a consistent basis. It's that consistent public awareness that encourages sponsors to endorse a program, advertisers to buy in, publishers to take the next book, manufacturers to seek an endorsement, and even the public to tune in! That's how celebrity equals cash flow.

My advice was seldom, if ever, taken. I was looked upon as Graham's wife again, not a producer, although I had won two Emmy nominations as daytime producer of the year for two years running. I was given the title of production consultant; however, I was only consulted once or twice. Graham and I would discuss things before we went to the studio, and he would put them into practice. Sometime later, in the editing of the program, I did have quite a lot of input. Again, through all these pro-grams, as in the Galloping Gourmet *days, I felt rejected and received little recognition. However, during this stressful time, I wrote a poem about being in the shadow and feeling rejected, and I learned yet another life lesson that I know helped my health. "All things work for good . . ." (Rom. 8:29).*

SUBSTANCE IN THE SHADOW
Shadows are different,
they seldom are warm.
Some are quite chilly, unpleasant, forlorn —
Especially when shadows come
from the fame
Of one who is known to the public by name.
Fixed quiet in shadow, obscure and unknown,
As a solitary substance, I stand there, alone.
I missed, fixed quietly in shadow, obscure
and unknown.
As a solitary substance, I stood there alone.
My festering feelings ranted and raved.
Ugly thoughts surged toward
those who rejected.
Vehemence and fury thrust with hostility
At the rudeness, ill manners,
and lack of urbanity.
Anger and pain caused my

substance to seethe.
(Rejection eclipses all love with such ease.)

My love in the limelight, always, knew
Of my anger and pain from within his shadow.
I majored on insults and slights, 'til the day
When I saw a figure, just a whisper away.
He was vaguely familiar to me, in a way.
Could it be? Was it? The Lord in the shade?
After all, the sacrifices He made.
No one but He ever had such rejection,
Yet, He forgave and loved with compassion.
Even today He's continually spurned
I must confess shame, for now that I see
He is the Substance in Shadow, not me.

During those fifteen years, we never regained the *Galloping Gourmet*'s celebrity; we simply edged along with our heads just above water. Nothing we did was apparently newsworthy or controversial. We were consistently searching for personal and public wellness, and that's pretty ho-hum to the media.

However, what was happening in our own lives was a wonderful test of that Scripture about all things turning together for good. Treena's health continued to improve until, after one stress test, they proclaimed her "40 percent fitter than the average woman of her age who hasn't had a stroke or a heart attack." We were delighted in her progress, which had now included the arrival of full-blown diabetes II (adult onset), with a fasting glucose of 380 (126 is considered the *start* point for diabetes II). Her AIC (a measurement of red blood cells taken every ninety days) was 11.9 and is now a 6. For every one point on that scale, there is a 30 percent less likelihood of another stroke or heart attack due to diabetes. Therefore, her risk potential dropped by 180 percent. We were thrilled — all the more so because we were living what we were teaching. We were consistent, and we had (to some degree) earned the respect of those who didn't share our faith. And therein, as Shakespeare once said, "lies the rub." Look once again at this Scripture:

"Make it your ambition to lead a quiet life,
to mind your own business and to work
with your hands, . . . so that your daily life
may win the respect of outsiders
and so that you will not be dependent on
anybody."
1 THESSALONIANS 4:11–12 NIV

I took to these verses like a duck to water. I wasn't exactly leading a quiet life, but I was using my hands, minding my own business, and we had earned a measure of respect and had eventually paid off all our debts. We were obligated to no man.

So weren't we biblically correct?

Like, isn't vitamin C the same as an orange?

I was to learn that "isolated Scripture" in self-serving hands is almost as unreliable as statistics.

CHAPTER THIRTY-THREE: SECOND PLACE

*Back to the crossroads from whence
we'd made a detour,
From Jesus Without Compromise
to logic and it's tenure.
God had to take again first place and
we became mature
By taking second place to God
where we had been before.*

My dear friend Julia Child, a true celebrity who was so well known for what she actually did (and how she spoke), used to say in that rich New England pitch, "You can eat anything if you eat it in moderation." To which I would respond, "Yes, Julia, but how do you measure what is moderate?" In another context, the one we are exploring in this book, how does one *measure* being a *consistent witness* of what Jesus Christ did, what He said, and what He continues to do in and through us as individuals who have chosen to follow after Him? I would measure my consistency during those fifteen years as a 40/10. That ratio represents 40 percent in my private, personal life and 10 percent in my publicly observable life. Notice, if you will, that these are an assessment of my life, not Treena's. Her witness was intact. Mine were not good numbers for someone called upon to love God, neighbor, and self with 100 percent of my heart, soul, and mind!

So in the midst of Treena's healing and God's gracious repair of our finances, I had, in fact, lived out my Christian life below the surface of general public awareness. In part I had not lived, as we had initially declared, for "Jesus without compromise." All this was about to change, the detour was almost over, and we were back at the crossroads on the way to outdulgence.

During the fifteen-year detour we had obviously worked very hard, sometimes under difficult, oppressive circumstances. We had needed a place apart, a respite during the great Pacific Northwest summers, surely among the best anywhere on earth. We found a small sailboat called a "Nonesuch." At first we had a thirty-footer, and then a thirty-six that we called "Dovetail."

She became our place apart for which we were extremely grateful. We would count off the days until we were free to jump aboard and almost disappear into our own space.

This was to be a wonderful time of relaxation for my Gra, and I truly loved it when we were anchored in a quiet place, away from the waves and the wind.

I've told you how I disliked sailing, but when I saw the joy on Gra's face, it was worth any sacrifice. I don't want you to think I was "special" or anything. I wasn't. I just loved Graham and knew this was the only way he could relax. We were so close to God's creation, and it gave ample opportunity for prayer and trusting Jesus to guide us. I was also able to write some poetry and paint a few pictures. God helped me take the very best advantage of this sailing time. I was really happy.

It's hard for me to admit that owning a sailboat isn't *exactly* good stewardship, but then again it is a wonderful example of God's grace!

When we went aboard, we really felt we were in the midst of this loving, healing provision for us both. When the wind picked up, it was a gift for me, and when it dropped it was a gift for Treena! In 2002, while anchored in Annette Inlet in the Gulf Islands during an incredibly beautiful (but windless) September, I went up to lie out in our furled mainsail. I've always read or written or slept out in the sun. I'd never gone out to simply listen. It was in that sail, during that month, that I began to hear God talking about second place.

Perhaps I had never really ever listened before, and that is odd because throughout our Christian lives Treena has spoken publicly and practiced privately this very special gift. I'm prepared to admit that I've been too busy searching for *measurable* results — too impressed with logical straight edges and things that work, thus proving that they qualify as being right. I'd become a man of prayer because it had been well proven to me that this presuming upon God fitted in with my plans. Such an approach was . . . well, stupid. But to *listen* — just listen without asking for specific direction on a pressing issue? Unlikely, until the late summer of 2002.

At sixty-eight years of age I went out to sit in the furled sail without a book or a pencil and pad. I went out to simply listen to whatever I might be told. Turn on a small portable

FM/AM radio receiver almost anywhere on earth and you'll hear voices, and yet there is no evidence of the speaker to be seen. The words are invisible yet they are everywhere. So, we believe, is God's communication everywhere to all those who will take the time to listen. Some tough cases (like me) may need a place apart on a sailboat in summer, but I'm convinced that a Greyhound bus seat on a red-eye trip is equally valid to the one who sets out, without any agenda, *to listen*.

Among the things I thought I might have heard that day and that I have borne with me since that day were four words: *settle into second place*. I wanted more understanding. Mostly I wanted to screen out any potential to be self-serving. The one thing I really knew about me was my ability to initiate, innovate, and generally complicate the simplest of all issues. I wanted what Oliver Wendell Holmes wanted and was prepared to give his life for — "simplicity on the other side of complexity."

I would like to share with you part of a lecture I developed after reading a book called Bottom Line *by T. H. Harrell. He wrote this:*

"An average speaker speaks   *125–160 words per minute.*

An average listener hears   *400 to 500 words per minute.*

Normal listeners retain   *7–9% of what they have heard.*

They remember only   *25% of that 7–9%.*

They forget half of that in   *8 hours."*

I worked out how many words we would re-member from a twenty-minute sermon. Some go longer, I know, but remember, we are taking the average. Thus,

An average sermon lasts approx. 20 minutes   *2,500 words*

We receive   *9% = 225 words*

We remember   *25% = 56 words*

We forget   *1/2 = 28 words*

On Monday we may recall   *14 words. [Poor pastor!]*

Taking the average words spoken (125) from the potential 400 words heard leaves a 275-word space. I believe this 275-word space is God-given and we misuse it. I believe nothing about us is ever wasted, and that this appar-ent gap is actually a spiritual receiver through which the Holy Spirit wants to transmit convic-

tion, revelation, understanding, wisdom, guidance, challenge, and/or comfort. However, this space is usually filled with what I call "butterfly" thoughts, e.g., "I've heard all this before." "How long has he/she been married?" "Hope they don't take long, it's such a lovely day outside." "The roast is burning." "Betsy should hear this. It would do her good. I'll get her a tape."

But what is God saying to YOU? These thoughts clutter up the reception through which we might have received from the Lord!

We need to clear our 275-word space of all anxieties, worries about children, and how you're going to manage. If we can hear all God has for us, then maybe we would hear Him solve one of our problems.

He has a reason for you being there, so listen. Listen WHEREVER you go.

We returned that summer with those four words — "settle into second place" — and not much more understanding. That would have to come in God's good timing. It was between the summer of 2002 and 2003 that the word *outdulgence* arrived as a descriptor of the earlier vision. If we had not experienced the stroke, the heart attack, the diabetes, and all the research and healing of those fifteen years, I really doubt that we would ever have grasped the idea of outdulgence as a godly means of serving others at such a time as this. We had suffered pain and sickness firsthand. We had seen the consequences of legalism, rebellion, indulgence, and compromise. We had discovered the long-term blessings of doing a small thing and doing it well until it was done. We had seen how those small changes in our lives could help others in theirs.

We were ready to be of service. The vision finally made all kinds of sense. It was time to rejoin His highway.

I was ready, absolutely, to be released to serve at last. I was getting very excited. I had waited so long, and at last it looked like I might be able to teach again! To be set apart to listen to the Lord, what a joy. There is a wonderful little poem that Hannah Whitall Smith wrote:

> *To sit and think of God —*
> *O what a Joy it is*
> *To think the thought,*
> *To breathe the name.*
> *Earth has no greater Bliss.*

The summer of 2003 was even more glorious than 2002, but then that may well have been an "attitude" thing. We agreed that this time we'd try something out in a practical manner. We would see what it was like to settle into second place — while sailing!

We had sailed almost thirty thousand miles in thirty years, and the last ten years had been spent in the Pacific Northwest. We knew our way around and had visited almost every marina and hundreds of inlets. This time we would settle into second place and let Him (Jesus) *lead*. This was to *allow* Him to *invade* an area of personal proficiency into which there were few, if any, moral or ethical issues at stake. Really, what did it matter if we went into Sidney Harbor or on to Ganges, when the weather was the only *real* issue? We wound up in Silva Bay, a small boating community on the western shores of the Georgian Straight amid the Canadian Gulf Islands. Treena was ashore for the day, and I was left alone with the leak.

We had a simple twelve-volt pressure pump to push our domestic water supply from faucet to faucet. It had worked for ten years just fine, but somewhere lurking below the cabin floor there had developed a slow leak that made the noisy pressure pump run for a second or so for no apparent purpose. I went to the small boatyard to get help (I'm not much good at technical repairs), but nobody was available until much later that day. I returned to the increasingly irritating pump, but it was getting much worse. I decided to give it a go — to try to fix it *myself.*

I rolled up the fitted carpet, unscrewed the fifty-six screws (so who is obsessive-compulsive?), and lifted up the entire flooring when bingo, the last piece revealed the leak at a junction for hot water under the galley. I tightened up the plastic nut carefully until the leak *stopped.* It stopped — I'd fixed it *myself.* Yeah! I replaced all the flooring and *all* the fifty-six screws, put the carpet back, and listened to the *silence* coming from the pump. When Treena returned, I could barely contain myself.

"Listen," I urged.

"To what?" she asked.

"Just listen," I repeated with a huge grin.

"I can't hear anything." She held her head to one side.

"That's the whole point," I chortled.

"What's the point?"

I decided not to press my luck any further. "The leak — the pump — I *fixed* it!" I was now literally jumping up and down with the sheer pleasure of achievement. I explained what I'd done, fifty-six screws and all, and, "Wow, isn't that great?" And then my beloved was once again used to transform my entire life with one question: "Did you pray?"

"Oh, well . . . I mean . . . it was only a little water leak. Surely it's not . . ." I simply petered out. We had decided to settle into second place and let Him lead, but I hadn't. I'd gone first again.

The next day I overfilled our diesel engine and needed to withdraw a couple of pints. I tried using a small suction pump to no avail. "Did you pray?" I could almost hear Treena's words again, so this time I prayed.

"Lord, I need your help, please!" I breathed. I was leaning into the engine compartment on my knees (appropriate?). It was almost as though He had joined me and was very close. Then came the whispered instruction. "The tube is in too deep. Take it out, measure it against the dip stick, and return it." I did exactly as told, and it worked. I was pleased, *but I wasn't as pleased as I had been when I'd fixed the leak.*

I'd repaired the leak all on my own, and my *self* had rejoiced at my success. In the latter case I'd asked for help, and I couldn't take the credit. It struck me suddenly and completely. My whole life had been an almost endless confirmation of selfish cause and effect, both success and failure. It had all been about me and my choices. With the leak I had reveled in success, but my faith hadn't moved one iota. With the oil I had less successful feelings, but my faith had risen considerably. Could this be what He means by "settling into second place"?

Isn't it also true that oil and water cannot mix!

Now perhaps I might be ready to serve, but there was one more issue to be settled, one that was far more complex than oil and water. This issue had seriously limited the Christian church for literally hundreds of years. It was that old social justice and evangelism issue, and it was alive and unwell in our own marriage. Treena, as you have no doubt gathered by this time, is no pushover, and yet from her earliest days of faith she has bided her time — or rather waited on God's timing — before raising troublesome issues.

It was now the right time.

Treena understood about the need for relinquishment of habits that harmed. Had she not given up a stage and film career because of its potential to harm our marriage? Had she not repeated the loss of her second career in New Zealand in order to produce *Galloping Gourmet* (which she genuinely hated to do)? Had she not had to hand over our third child, Kareena, to a full-time nanny in order to complete the production task? Had she not endured thirty thousand miles under sail, most of which scared her to death because she'd almost drowned twice as a child? And finally, in the midst of her newly acquired and joyfully embraced teaching career within the Christian community, that had been so well received in the creative lifestyle group and around the world, this too had been dislodged by the ever-present "celebrity-first" pressures of the media.

Yes, I was excited, a real blessing from our Lord. I was ready. Eventually, things work out perfectly, especially when both sides in a Christian marriage work together to be of service, both to the Lord and His people. I have found this to be truth. Yes, it is a struggle to begin with, but it is worth the struggle in honor preferring the other. That is the answer, if we can both keep that engraved on our hearts. For when we both give together, Jesus can be seen between us. We try to be like Aquila and Priscilla. Graham will sometimes — well, most times — lead, or I may. It is up to the Lord. We call it couple power.

And so now, here we were again, with a whole new experience, another opportunity for her to once again use her gifting. She could help to provide the essential inner understanding of the deep healing needed before one embraces the more easily *measured* exchange of habits for social justice. The great ugly chasm that has divided the church for generations and confused the world about her collective inconsistencies now needed to be confronted *honestly* in our own lives before we could ever hope to serve others.

CHAPTER THIRTY-FOUR: NOW THE RUBBER MEETS THE ROAD

*The rubber meets the road in more
ways than one;
this should be no surprise.
In more ways than one, we've had
"nine lives."
In this one we harmonize.*

Whatever we might do, we knew that we would *both* have to *settle into second place.* This would not be a matter of collecting straight edges and completing a puzzle. This was a puzzle that we had not begun and we would not finish. That had been started by others with far more experience than ours, and yet we were ourselves two small pieces, each with strengths and weaknesses, and each with evangelism and social justice in our hearts. *We* needed to fit, and in our witness *together* to be complete.

Ever since my return home in March 1975 as a "newly minted" Christian, we have prayed together every single night for what must now be more than eleven thousand days. I mention this not to gain your approval but rather to underscore how normal it has become for us to talk things out with God. It has also become normal (even though *awesomely* normal) to expect to hear back *if* we *listen*. We began by hearing God say, "It is time." We were anticipating that there would become a time when we were to relinquish the boat. On September 15, 2003, it happened just as we stood off Sidney Harbor Marina awaiting our turn to tie up alongside. Within the hour we received an idea. This time it wasn't a word — just a thought. We would replace "Dovetail" with a recreational vehicle that would combine our "place apart" with a way to go out into the world, this time without the constraint of short summer seasons. We had absolutely no experience driving anything larger than a small U-haul for a few hundred miles. All we knew was that it fitted our need to be known more as servants than celebrities.

We would not be flying into big cities to strut our stuff. We might be able to go to small townships and somehow be used to sow the seed of an idea. We prayed earnestly over several months about this thought, and then, one day, we believe that we were given our answer. We've shared this with others we respect as we now share it with you.

I didn't really believe it — no more sailing, no more television. I would be able to go back to full-time ministry with my darling Graham. This surely sounded like God to me.

Sprinkling seed like "Johnny Appleseed." What a joy! I knew only too well that God's ways are not our ways; however, I had prepared just in case and gathered all my lecture materials, poems for a new book to be called The One and Only *(which I still haven't had time to write). As I said, God works in His ways, not mine. Moreover, I've never been disappointed. (No, that's a lie, I have!) However, I do know that His ways are always the best and that one cannot second-guess Him. Therefore, off we go, this time after prayer and, we strongly believe, with His blessings.*

We saw ourselves as children again, about the time we just met, when we were ten and eleven years old. I watched as we held hands and skipped off down a country road. We laughed at each other as our pockets spilled seeds out in all directions. They never seemed to cease as they scattered. And then came the words to explain the picture: "Remember how it was when you met — your freedom to laugh and the awakening of love in your hearts. At that time you had a hole in your pocket (that was true because I kept losing my lunch money). You are to fill your pockets with my seed. I have plenty, and wherever you go you will let it freely cascade. Do not choose where to go; I will lead you. Do not watch the seed germinate or grow or bear fruit — that is yet for others. You are to simply sow the idea as you skip off on the road together."

We were to go out as young children and spill out the seed of an idea, an idea that might spring forth as the riverbank trees in Ezekiel 47. Their fruit was for food and their leaves were for healing — surely social justice and healing — and everywhere that the river flowed it brought life!

CHAPTER THIRTY-FIVE: THE SEED, THE WHOLE SEED, AND NOTHING BUT THE SEED

King's Kids, sowing seed as we
skip toward the finish line.
Seed may grow, seed may die,
seed may never multiply,
But seed that falls on fertile soil
will produce a crop divine —
A 100, 60, 30 times which we sow to glorify.

In Jesus' time, a particular fig tree was used as a metaphor to describe the temple wherein Jesus could find no fruit. He actually cursed the fruitless tree, and within the day, it died from the roots *up!*

I invite you to read through the Bible and keep your eyes open for the trees, the vines, and the plants. It's an amazing series of accounts. Such small self-contained beginnings — a seed, a nut, a pit — and from its very completeness springs forth a sometimes enormous tree. The small becomes big in God's time.

Today the church, after more than two thousand years of growth, is huge. The question is, where's the fruit?

We need to ask that, not of the church universal, but of that unique "planting of the Lord," that "tree of righteousness" that we attend. Does it bear fruit in season, and is there healing in its sheltering leaves?

Over the years, in an effort to provide unique services or programs, some churches have attempted novel forms of gene-splicing in which they have genetically altered the original seed in order to upgrade its appearance. They have spliced these slices of worldly marketing DNA into the gospel and changed its fruit in such a subtle way that we may be unaware of exactly what we are consuming.

It just looks good to eat.

Treena and I certainly don't want you to imagine for a moment that we seriously see our marriage as a model for the modern church. However, we do see our *willingness* to face our shortcomings and our *passion* to improve as a healthy alternative to becoming comfortable with plastic fruit.

And I would like to add plastic flowers. So many times we act like plastic flowers, with no perfume and phony exteriors that can take folks in for awhile.

We all need to flourish as if in God's Love Garden, to bring Him delight. We are living plantings in His garden, and tragically we seem to have an attack of aphids, which manifest as criticism, a cancer in the body of Christ.

We often destroy each other with critical words when we are supposed to love our neighbors as Jesus loved us, and even to love ourselves. I believe strongly that if we saw ourselves as a flower, tree, herb, or even a weed in God's garden, that we would begin to delight in our unique blooms, every one of us a testimony to His creativity.

Are we a garden of delight to our Lord? We can be if we listen. We have a wonderful Gardener who nourishes us with words, each one a seed, this time for His garden in our hearts.

Treena longs to provide the spiritual understanding that must come hand-in-glove with physical healings that *last*. I long to provide the raw materials and lasting compassionate connections that validate the teachings about a God of love. We see that one without the other is not a whole seed. When the two are one, there is both fruit for food and leaves for healing. Wherever these plantings are watered by God's river of love, there is the provision of life that does not wither or fail.

Time and time again within this book we've talked about cash flow and related it to a mudflow or even a mudslide. These human phenomena are in direct opposition to God's river of life and love that is *specifically* free from the love of money (which can also be defined as a preoccupation with cash flow).

My responsibility as a husband and father is to provide for my own family, and if I fail to do so, then it would be worse for me than for an unbeliever. That's part of the good seed, and it demands my attention. But must it dominate my thinking and planning as it has on many an occasion in my past?

In the same way, must a church budget or a missionary support dominate the thinking of its servant leaders?

We think not!

Our simple task is to be observed as a set-apart people, a people who see themselves as *settled into second place* with Jesus in the lead. As such, we become witnesses to His words and His deeds through us as we seek to serve our broken, weeping, and lost world.

Inevitably, a seed that seeks to grow into such a fruit-bearing tree will be forced to compare itself with another type of tree that grows in the middle of the garden — the one from which, if we eat, we shall surely die. And yet its fruit has all the *appearance* of being a delight to the palate and the ego.

In the end, it isn't about numbers. Certainly there are whole seed plantings that have grown to gargantuan size and still bear much fruit, but this does not mean that the small vine does not provide equal sweetness and healing.

It isn't about numbers because in the midst of those numbers can be free radicals that damage the DNA messengers and weaken individual cells of faith and bring about the cancers of criticism and division that so wound the body of Christ in our time.

Treena and I want to be free of such deadly influences, and yet we long to make a vital contribution to the health, well-being, and effectiveness of the modern Christian church. We have tried our best to discuss one such division that has flourished over the past two hundred years — the "great ugly chasm" between the conservative evangelical and the liberal social justice. We have tried to build a bridge over this chasm by starting, first of all, in our own lives and marriage.

It certainly hasn't been easy. We've had this

debate many times, so it's no wonder there is such division within Christendom. How sad when Jesus did it all. He fed, He healed, and He taught the gospel of the kingdom of God. His love overflowed into the hearts that were willing to hear.

As much as I yearn to feed the hungry and to work for peace and reconciliation, I must understand that there are forces buried deeply within me that are profoundly ungodly. Without the consistent exposure to God's Word and the salt, light, and salvation that it brings, I'm likely to wind up *once again* in a hole of my own making. When I *hear* what Treena has to say to the church, I become increasingly aware of how much I need to *listen.*

I need to pray. I need to settle. I need to forgive. I need to confess. I need to submit. I need to sacrifice. Oh, how needy I am for all that the conservative churches can provide.

Perhaps one day I can be whole as I hold onto the hand of the one who loves me and skip off down the roadway spilling *whole* seeds in every direction.

May there be much fruit and leaves for healing on either side of the river of Your love, Lord.

The highway is before us. We have begun

to settle into second place for the longest unplanned trip we've ever made.

We have an idea to share in seed form.

We have been told to keep refilling our pockets and not to bother about repairing the holes. The seed is meant to spill everywhere.

We have been told not to concern ourselves with where the seeds fall or how they germinate or grow, or even how they might bear fruit.

Our task is to hold hands, skip, laugh, and sing until it's time to go home.

We are to give up being concerned about cash flow and muddy waters because it is our task to swim upstream into increasingly clear, unpolluted streams. We are to relinquish our home and invest in the homeless and hopeless, and with our motor home we are to be content.

Above all, we are to settle into second place and be consistent witnesses of His everlasting love for us and for our broken world.

Come skip with us in Second Place,
And spread your seed just everyplace.
Don't be concerned where seeds may fall.
It's nothing to do with you at all.
Time is running out, it's true.
Can you hear Him calling you?

Come skip with us; don't be afraid.
Just give before all love doth fade.
Preserve your hearts and soul, dear friend,
With compassions and joy which has no end.
Come skip with us in Second Place,
For soon we'll see Him face-to-face.

APPENDIX A
LIST OF NGOS

SERVING PEOPLE WHO ARE HUNGRY

Childcare International — Our focus is upon meeting the needs of the poor, with emphasis on children, through a social, medical, and spiritual ministry based upon the gospel of Jesus Christ. (800-553-2328)

> www.childcare-intl.org,
> info@childcare-intl.org

City Team Ministries — City Team Ministries is a nonprofit organization serving the poor and homeless in San Jose, San Francisco, Oakland, Portland, Seattle, Philadelphia, and partnerships in more than seven other countries around the world. (408-232-5600)

> www.cityteam.org, info@cityteam.org

Community Harvest Food Bank, Indiana — Of the 23.3 million needy people seeking emergency food assistance in the U.S., more than 9 million are children. (260-447-3696)

www.communityharvest.org,
info@communityharvest.org

Compassion International — Releasing children from poverty in Jesus' name. (800-336-7676)   www.compassion.com

Heifer International — Ending Hunger, Caring for the Earth (800-422-0474)

www.heifer.org

MEDA — Mennonite Economic Development Associates' goal for the hungry is to provide people with the tools and means to feed themselves and their families. (MEDA's vision is that all people may experience Christ's love and utilize their abilities to earn a livelihood, provide for families, and enrich their communities. Its mission: As an association of Christians, in business and the professions, committed to applying biblical teachings in the marketplace, MEDA members share their faith, abilities, and resources to address human needs through economic development.) (800-665-7026)

www.meda.org

Samaritan's Purse — We offer hope. To suffering people in a broken world, we share the news of the only One who can bring true peace: Jesus Christ, the Prince of Peace.   www.samaritanspurse.org

World Concern — In the hardest places in the world, among families in greatest need, we are doing what matters most. (425-771-5700)   www.worldconcern.org, info@worldconcern.org

World Vision — World Vision is a Christian relief and development organization dedicated to helping children and their communities worldwide reach their full potential by tackling the causes of poverty. (888-511-6548)   www.worldvision.org

SERVING PEOPLE WHO ARE THIRSTY

Clean Water for Haiti — Clean Water for Haiti is working to help those with extreme needs in the country of Haiti.
www.cleanwaterforhaiti.org, info@cleanwaterforhaiti.org

SERVING PEOPLE WHO ARE EXPOSED

City Union Mission — City Union Mission offers emergency help, long-term hope, and opportunities for the future. In all of our programs the life-changing good news of Jesus is lovingly shared with each person. (816-474-9380)

www.cumission.org, info@cumission.org

I.M.P.A.C.T. — International Missions Projects and Construction Teams is a Christ-centered ministry providing individuals and groups with practical short-term missions opportunities designed to fulfill the Great Commission. (425-378-7740)

www.impact-ministries.org, impact@impact-ministries.org

Union Rescue Mission — Beginning as a gospel wagon, URM has been serving the poor and homeless of Los Angeles for 113 years. (213-347-6300) www.urm.org

Serving People Who Are "Exiled"

Refugees International — A Powerful Voice for Lifesaving Action. (202-828-0110) www.refintl.org, ri@refintl.org

The Salvation Army — The Salvation Army, an international movement, is an evangelical part of the universal Christian Church. Its message is based on the Bible.

Its ministry is motivated by the love of God. Its mission is to preach the gospel of Jesus Christ and to meet human needs in His name without discrimination.

www.salvationarmy.org

SERVING PEOPLE WHO ARE SICK

American Leprosy Missions — Christ's servants, freeing the world of leprosy.

www.leprosy.org

Boyer Children's Clinic — Serving children with cerebral palsy and other developmental delay for more than sixty years. We improve the quality of life of children with neuromuscular disorders or other developmental delays by providing the best solutions for each child and family. (306-325-8477)

www.boyercc.org,
information@boyercc.org

Christian Medical & Dental Association — The Christian Medical & Dental Associations exist to motivate, educate, and equip Christian physicians and dentists to glorify God by: living out the character of Christ in their homes, practices, communities and around the world; pursuing professional competence and Christ-like compassion in their daily work; influencing their families, colleagues, and patients toward a right relationship with Jesus Christ; advancing biblical principles in bioethics and health to the Church and society. (888-231-2637)

www.cmdahome.org,
main@cmdahome.org

MAP International — MAP's three-fold mission is to provide essential medicines, prevent and eradicate disease, and promote community health development. MAP's international programs are eliminating the causes of sickness and disease by providing free medicines and medical care, improving water supplies and food production, and establishing community directed health education and training. (912-265-6010)

www.map.org, map@map.org

March of Dimes — The mission of the March of Dimes is to improve the health of babies by preventing birth defects and infant mortality.

www.modimes.org

MEDA — Mennonite Economic Development Associates. We are finding ways to sustainably bring health services, medicines, and products to the rural poor in Africa and other parts of the world. (800-665-7026)   www.meda.org

Medical Ambassadors International — Transforming nations community by community; now serving in more than sixty countries. (888-403-0600)
www.medicalambassadors.org

The Smile Train — This train delivers hope — and new smiles — to desperate children all around the world. (212-689-9199)
www.SmileTrain.org,
info@SmileTrain.org

SERVING PEOPLE WHO ARE IMPRISONED

Bridge Builders for Kids — Bridge Builders for Kids is an Evangelical Christian ministry that serves children of prisoners. (651-345-5441)
www.bridgebuilders.cc,
steve@bridgebuilders.cc

Prison Fellowship — Exhorting, equipping, and assisting the church in its ministry to prisoners, ex-prisoners, and their families.
www.pfm.org

Prison Fellowship International — PFI is the global association of national Prison Fellowship (PF) organizations. (703-481-0000)

www.pfi.org, info@pfi.org

SERVING PEOPLE WHO ARE WIDOWED

Access, Inc. — Access, Inc., exists to build a caring community, through partnerships, that has the courage to shape its own future.

www.access-inc.org

Families Northwest — Making the Northwest the world's premier place for marriage, family life, and children.

www.familiesnorthwest.org

Focus on the Family — To cooperate with the Holy Spirit in disseminating the gospel of Jesus Christ to as many people as possible, and, specifically, to accomplish that objective by helping to preserve traditional values and the institution of the family.

www.family.org

MEDA — Mennonite Economic Development Associates' goal for widows is to provide women with the tools and means to provide economically for themselves and their families. (800-665-7026)

www.meda.org

Serving People Who Are Orphaned

African Children's Choir — Helping Africa's most vulnerable children today, so they can help Africa tomorrow.

www.africanchildrenschoir.com

Children to Love — Children to Love International (CLI) was formed in 1993 to reach orphaned and abandoned children in Romania with the gospel of Christ. (661-588-9000)

www.childrentolove.com,
ctl@childrentolove.com

Children's Choice Foster Care, Kinship & Adoption Services — Children's Choice provides community based, specialized Christian services, as a bridge for individuals who are in need of the reintegrative processes of family living. Intensive, individual, supportive casework counseling services empower clients to achieve their highest potential as responsible citizens. (800-522-4453)

www.childrenschoice.org

MEDA — Mennonite Economic Development Associates are finding ways to enable children to work and go to school, bringing hope for a long-term career that can sustain themselves. (800-665-7026)

www.meda.org

APPENDIX B
DRAFT LETTER
OF COMMITMENT

Dear [Try to find a real person to address!]

We have decided to provide support to your agency for the next three years, commencing [_____] and concluding on [_____]. Our details are attached.

If we decide to discontinue funding on [_____], we will give you one year's advance notice and will include our reason(s) for not going forward.

We have based our decision on the ideas contained in the book *Recipe for Life: Converting Habits That Harm into Resources That Heal* (Nashville, Tenn.: Broadman & Holman Publishers) and Graham and Treena Kerr's Web site: www.outdulgence.com.

While our abundance can become a supply for others' needs (through your agency), we also believe *strongly* that we will need to receive feedback from the "point of need" as an encouragement, as we wrestle with past habits.

Please see 2 Corinthians 8:14 to underscore the issue of "spiritual equality" between donor and recipient.

We look forward to being active partners with you in reaching out to those in need.

Thank you for being there at a time like this.

With Sincerity, [or your sign-off]

STOP PRESS!

Our efforts to serve via the media and specifically through the "Gathering Place" television series are now being pressed into a new mold, for which we are deeply grateful. On page 296 we comment that the series sold . . . *just!* It would now appear that it has new life as a series of DVDs.

As a result of all the years of wiser lifestyle choices, combined with the excellent advice showered upon us by so many medical authorities (our guests on the series), we have discovered a new way to order our inner and outer lives and so be more effective in our Christian service to others in need. We call it lifestyle #9, and we are hard at work (during the winter months) writing a very practical lifestyle/cookbook that embodies outdulgence and the four sets of goals needed to help apply the up to eighty-one hours of real entertainment and information contained in the DVD series.

The new cookbook is provisionally titled *Lifestyles for a Lifetime Cookbook.* The new DVD series is called "Graham and Treena Kerr's Lifestyle #9." You can learn more about both and their availabilities on www .grahamkerr.com.

G & T

P.S. We are still very much in second place!

ABOUT THE AUTHORS

Graham Kerr was born in London, England, and developed his famous "Galloping Gourmet" television series in New Zealand, Australia, and Canada before it was distributed to a worldwide audience of two hundred million. He is a landmark chef, best-selling author, and a former Youth With A Mission missionary, ordained elder, and pastor now dedicated to full-time ministry with his wife Treena.

Treena Kerr was born in Dover, England, and pursued an early career in professional theater. An Emmy-nominated producer and published poet, she now serves in full-time ministry with her husband to whom she has been married for fifty years. The Kerrs now live in Washington State.